Karl Martin's passion for Jesus Christ is infectious. He
has built up one of Britain's most exciting and innovative
churches through prayer, vision, determination and a
longing for more people to experience the love of God for
themselves.

Nicky Gumbel

We need voices that proclaim in a non-preachy and helpful
manner what a person of God looks like and how to become
one. Therein lies power to exceed normal. I'm thankful that
this book gives access to that power that all of us long for.

Brian Tome

Karl Martin lives what he believes, he is also a brilliant
communicator. In this practical and engaging book Karl
gives us a glimpse of the radical Christian life, and a taste
for living it to the full.

Amy Orr-Ewing

Karl has written a book that manages a rare combination:
being both profoundly rooted in Scripture and completely
drenched in real life experience. It is a passionate call and
profoundly practical pathway to the original practice and
call of Jesus: discipleship.

Mike Breen

stand

stand.

KARL MARTIN

Muddy
Pearl

First published in 2013 by
Muddy Pearl, Edinburgh, Scotland.
www.muddypearl.com
books@muddypearl.com

British Library Cataloguing in Publication Data
A catalogue record for this book is available from the British Library

ISBN 978 1 910012 03 1

Typeset by Waverley Typesetters, Warham
Printed in Great Britain by Bell & Bain Ltd, Glasgow

To Lydia, Keziah, Abi and Esther, you are the joy of my life.

And to Nicola, you improve me, support me, complete me and provoke me to follow Jesus. I love you.

Contents

Stand out, Stand by

Stand Back

Foreword

The first time I stayed at his house, Karl Martin was carrying around a gnarly, old, leather shoulder bag. It went everywhere with him; carried his laptop, Bible, journal, bundles of paper. That bag came straight out of the 1930s. It had a moss green lining, was small enough to tuck under his arm, big enough for an overnighter, and manly enough not to be mistaken for a lady's handbag. I liked it. In fact I'd been looking for one just like it online, I'd visited specialist stores, and had even emailed a leatherworker in Wisconsin for a quote.

'Nice bag', I said.

'You like it?'

'Where did you get it?'

'Scottish company. Ethically sourced. Hand-stitched . . . Here.'

Without warning Karl suddenly inverted the bag. A small avalanche of papers fell out and then with a thud his old dog-eared Bible did the splits onto the table too. 'Have it', he grinned.

I stammered my protest but he just wouldn't listen.

'Mate, it'll give me an excuse to get a new one.'

The next time I saw Karl he was carrying his stuff around in a plastic carrier bag, and I was carrying mine in a gnarly, old leather number with moss green lining.

Karl didn't give me that bag on the off chance that I would one day blow his cover in the foreword to a book. He did it privately and impulsively because he's genuinely kind and a sacrificial.

I tell you this partly because the private lives of leaders matter, and partly because this book reads like a compelling extension of that one simple exchange. It's generous, authentic and challenging. Karl doesn't do trivial pursuits. He's a big-hearted, big-fisted, big picture kind of man, which is another way of saying that he's a leader. At a time when an entire generation is questioning Christianity, Karl fills his home with students and tells them they can change the world. Right now he's busy turning one of the bigger venues in Edinburgh into a centre for prayer, mission, enterprise and mercy. And in a nation where pastors are often afraid to pioneer, Karl is unashamedly planning to start loads of new congregations in every major city. Why? Because most people in those cities don't yet know Jesus, and most Christians in most churches don't yet know Jesus' plans for their lives.

● ● ●

A publisher once told me that Christians don't really read books on discipleship any more. This saddens me because Christ's whole message was a call to follow. Apparently we want books that make us feel nice. Pretty books. Books by famous authors. And sensationalised novels about the End Times, based on very dodgy theology. Well, *Stand* is unapologetically and defiantly an ancient, urgent call to Christian discipleship. And the fact that you are about to read it is significant. It shows that God is stirring something unusual in your heart – a longing for the kind of encounter with God that changes everything and the kind of obedience that changes the world. I believe that the Holy Spirit has placed this desire in you precisely because he plans to fulfil it. He's not setting you up to fail. He's brought you to this moment and this book in order to redefine normality and to propel you out on new adventures of faith.

It's time for this generation to take a stand for Jesus. To pray like it all depends on God, and to live like it all depends on us.

I don't know what that will look like for you – a new courage, a new direction, a new willingness to sacrifice everything for Jesus. *Stand* could well cost you big things like your time, your ambition, and your money, but also the little things of life, like the old leather bag, sitting beside me as I type.

Pete Greig
Guildford 2013

Thank you . . .

to Nicky Gumbel, Pete Greig, Mike Breen, Amy Orr Ewing for your encouragement.

to Justin Thacker and Mark Knight for your theological input.

to my extended family at Central, to my fathers and mothers, my brothers and sisters, my sons and daughters, you know who you are.

and to Mark and Richard and Stephanie without whom this would never have been.

Preface

Stand is an invitation to action. A provocation to involvement. Can true faith in God be passive? There are many moments in life where sit or lie or kneel or even run are entirely helpful instructions. However this book's concern is to cause an uprising, a pursuit of God and his purposes and a taking hold of life.

So stand.

Stand up. Stand firm. Stand free. Stand out.

> *I waited patiently for the LORD;*
> *   he turned to me and heard my cry.*
> *He lifted me out of the slimy pit,*
> *   out of the mud and mire;*
> *he set my feet on a rock*
> *   and gave me a firm place to stand.*
> *He put a new song in my mouth,*
> *   a hymn of praise to our God.*
>
> Psalm 40:1–3

Introduction

So, I read *The Heavenly Man*, by Brother Yun. An inspirational Christian biography. You know the kind. Inspirational. It reminds you how God is doing incredible things in our world today.

But it's also frustrating. Deeply.

Frustrating because this guy Brother Yun seems so ... holy. It is all, like: 'Memorise the whole Bible. Persevere through suffering. Expect miracles. Suffer some more. Expect more miracles.' Frustrating because I want to be completely holy. And I'm completely human.

I was inspired. And encouraged. I was definitely encouraged. And yet I felt somehow I wasn't going to like this guy, if I'm honest. Which is exactly what I intend to be.

Brother Yun shows up in Leeds, at a time when I'm pastor of a growing church there. My wife Niki and I head off to Leeds United's football stadium. And Brother Yun is AMAZING. He doesn't speak much English, so he preaches through an interpreter.

Brother Yun has a pretty unique preaching style. Throughout the course of his sermon, he keeps firing out challenges, altar calls, and opportunities to respond. And, after about four minutes, Brother Yun says something that sounds like: ****∧"*{&++++@@@****. His interpreter lady says: 'All those who need to repent of sins and welcome Jesus into hearts right now – come to front.' They are a well-oiled machine.

And they come. In their scores. It's amazing.

But it's still frustrating.

Because it takes me forty minutes of carefully worded and pored over exposition to have any hope of seeing a response. And Brother Yun has said pretty much nothing!

Midway through the sermon, Brother Yun becomes more animated than ever. He launches into ""''''''**** ∧∧∧$ *****'''''''''@@@*** and the interpreter says: 'All those who are church leaders in City of Leeds come to front – NOW!!!!!'

I hate that. I do it to others. Pretty mercilessly, really. But I hate it. I'm at the back and I'm staying there. Niki looks at me and jabs me in the side with her account-ability elbow. She says nothing. But she means: 'Everyone else is going – half your church is up there – you'd better do as he says.'

Maturely, I shake my head.

Niki digs me again. Resistance over. I STAND.

Brother Yun calls out, '@@@****_____********'''''''''''$$$££@@@'.

And his interpreter calls out: 'All those who have a problem with pornography come to front NOW!'

I am the only one standing.

At this moment, I have a decision to make. Do I sit down really quickly, looking like a little boy caught with his hand deep in the sweetie jar? Or, do I man up and walk down to the front?

In case you're wondering: I have issues. Pornography isn't one of them. But, there I am standing, and what am I to do?

I walk. The walk of shame.

I can see members of my congregation nudging each other. I know what they're thinking. 'Aha!' And they smile, pastorally. I walk. When I eventually get to the front, God meets with me. As I look back, I know that this was a defining moment in my ministry.

So here's the thing. I don't know whether you have discovered this for yourself yet, but I'm pretty sure you will. If you are willing to stand and make yourself vulnerable before the Lord, you'll find he has this habit of showing up. He will. Place yourself openly and absolutely in his hand and you can be sure he will not let you down. God loves it when you do that. Go out on a limb with him. When you do, the Holy Spirit always shows up.

Fact.

And one more thing. If you get to the end of this book and decide it was an interesting read – even a helpful read – I will not have done my job. Really. This book is only worth reading if it changes stuff. Changes us. Changes us so that we can stand – stand with Jesus, stand with complete confidence in who we are because we know who he is. Stand in prayer. Stand in battle, against the attack of the enemy. And stand for him, stand out for him, to serve and represent him.

Change. That's what needs to happen. And for that to be the case – we each have to play our part.

What does our part look like? It will be different for each one of us. But it simply means being faithful to who God has called us to be – and what God has called us to do. To stand. Which for me right now is, I think, at least in part, to write this book.

And your part? It could be to be ready to listen. To open yourself up to what God might want to say to you. To the possibility that God wants to reveal himself to you in a new way, and perhaps even to transform you – inside out – so much so, that the transformation he does in you, he will also do through you. You will be able to stand on your own two feet in the light of his truth and give glory to him.

Are you up for this?

——————————————— SO: ———————————————

Would you join me in a prayer?

Place your hand on your ears.

Lord, thank you that you speak today. Will you inform and renew me in a fresh way. Will you change and reinforce my thinking with your truths.

Place your hand on your head.

Lord, thank you for my mind. Would you reveal yourself to me through your living word. Would you reveal yourself in a new way, as I make myself vulnerable to your Spirit.

Place your hand on your heart.

Lord would you transform this life. May I see the way you see. May I feel the way you feel. Can I move according to your purpose.

In Jesus name.

Amen.

PART 1.

THE STAND-IN

●

'I am Jesus, whom you are persecuting', the Lord replied. 'Now get up and stand on your feet. I have appeared to you to appoint you as a servant and as a witness of what you have seen and will see of me.'

Acts 26:15, 16

IF I WERE TO CALL YOU A STAND-IN YOU MIGHT WELL FEEL A LITTLE OFFENDED. I UNDERSTAND COMPLETELY. I'M NOT A STAND-IN OPTION OR A STAND-BY SOLUTION. I'M NOBODY'S STAND-IN, NOBODY'S REPLACEMENT.

BUT IF I WENT ON TO TELL YOU THAT YOUR CALLING AND PURPOSE AND ROLE IS TO STAND IN FOR JESUS, SAVIOUR OF THE WORLD, THAT IS ALTOGETHER A DIFFERENT THING AND POTENTIALLY, ALTOGETHER A DIFFERENT OFFENCE.

HE STOOD WHERE YOU WALK. HE WALKED SO YOU CAN STAND. IT'S ALL ABOUT THE STAND YOU MAKE. THE STAND YOU TAKE. YOU ARE THE STAND IN.

SO STAND.

YOUR STAND MAY WELL BE THE QUESTION, THE OPPORTUNITY, AND THE CHALLENGE OF YOUR LIFE.

1.

TRUE YOU

I'm fat, but I'm thin inside. Has it ever struck you that there's a thin man inside every fat man, just as they say there's a statue inside every block of stone?

Coming Up For Air, George Orwell (1939)

•

Today you are You, that is truer than true. There is no one alive who is Youer than You.

Happy Birthday to You!, Dr Seuss (1959)

•

For we are God's masterpiece. He has created us anew in Christ Jesus, so we can do the good things he planned for us long ago.

Ephesians 2:10 (NLT)

SOMETHING ABOUT ME

So, a while ago, things didn't feel right. The problem was me. It wasn't exclusively me, but it was enough me. At the age of thirty-four I had become the senior pastor of one of the largest Baptist churches in the country, and the problem was me. I wasn't confident that I wanted my life and I was pretty sure that nobody else would.

We had seventy-five students coming to a 6am discipleship class, we were teaching them the Bible and giving them bacon sandwiches and they were committing to reading through the New Testament in ten weeks and to becoming missional leaders. But I wasn't sure any of them would want my life. Certainly not enough for me to really disciple them.

We had over 300 students coming to an evening service and we were the best show in town. But I wasn't sure if what we were doing was really co-operating with the Holy Spirit of God. We'd just planted a new congregation with a postmodern vibe in the centre of the city and had stacks of people coming to it and I was leading them into new ways of doing church. But I wasn't sure that I knew what I was doing. Or where I was leading them.

I lacked a freedom to be who God had made me to be – to stand in the knowledge of who I was in him. I lacked a godly confidence to live for his approval. I lived far too much for the approval of others. The ambitions that God had given me had too easily become a personal ambition. Throughout my childhood I was encouraged to modify my volume and tone down my performance, sermons had taught me to modify behaviour, and it felt right. Theological college had encouraged me to modify my personality and church had forced me to modify my expectations and dress code and it felt odd, but that seemed to be what was required. All of this felt like medicine and jogging. You knew it was supposed to be good for you but it tasted bad and tired you out.

It left me doubting and wondering who I really was and what I was for, I was leading a church full of great people but the organisation, the institution, I didn't really like. It bored me, I felt restricted, like I had to conform, that I wasn't free, that what we were doing was good but perhaps not best. We talked an awful lot about things we were going to accomplish in God and didn't seem to achieve a lot. We were well-meaning but somehow not particularly effective.

So I did what I thought was right. I really believed it was what we had to do, I believed it with all of me. I mean, for goodness sake, I had prayed and sought the Lord. I was sure.

But others weren't. I had a clear vision, I could see how church could be, but I lacked the maturity and the mandate and the ability to convince a Baptist Church meeting.

It left me devastated. Unsure of what to do next.

At the time, I was unable to see that this was about what God was trying to do in me. So when Father God in his grace picked me up and moved me on, I thought the move was purely geographical. Actually, it was deeply spiritual. He called me to something new. And that new was less about the changes that would occur and the people I would lead. It was more about the transformation that needed to be done in me. I was to be freed to be who I was made to be.

See, I was born to lead. I am not a pastor and that is OK. I am a pioneer, prophet, preacher and apostle. I'm a broken one, but I am one nonetheless. I'm loud and spontaneous and I dream big dreams. I will have a go and I'll fail and I'll get it wrong and I'll upset people. But I have discovered that I am the most loved man in all the world.

I'm the best me that ever there was.

And so are you.

I will dress the way I dress. Only my wife and my girls will modify it and only occasionally.

And I will love Jesus.

And I will love his church.

And I am so desperate to lead his church out of anxiety and passivity and poverty and into its destiny – out of religion and into freedom – into the more that God has for us. God loves me and wants me to be me. God loves you and wants you to be you. And God has raised you and me up for such a time as this.

SOMETHING ABOUT YOU

There's something that I want you to hear. It's all about you. It's about becoming the real you. The true you. It's about becoming the true you and standing in the knowledge of who you are in him and really living.

It's all about you.

This is not something we hear very often in church. In fact it sounds rather counter-gospel. Because from the day we found faith we were taught firmly that it's not about us, it's about him. We heard sermons about the insidious dangers of the me-centred consumer culture, and sang worship songs that reminded us to forget about ourselves and concentrate on worshipping God. We came to church for a spiritual refill but were encouraged to leave our 'real' lives and our me-centred issues at the welcome desk as we came in. Because after all, it was not about us, it was about him.

Alarm bells are probably ringing as you read this. You could think I'm buying into one of the worst features of post-modernity. I don't mean that at all. This isn't about the enthronement of individualism.

It *is* about him. But it is also about you. In a big and incredibly important way. And these two things are not mutually exclusive.

See:

You are fearfully and wonderfully made.
You are absolutely known
           passionately loved
           pursued by Father God
           and paid for by Jesus
You are the body of Christ (at least part of it).
You are a child of the Father.
You are one in Christ.
You are filled with the Holy Spirit.
You are the salt of the earth.
You are the light of the world.

So it's about you. Because he loves you. He just loves you. And he wants you to know that – he wants to bring you fully back into relationship with him.

And it's about him.

And it's about the incredible calling he has for you to change the world.

But to stand with him in relationship, to stand in this incredible calling to the world, something needs to happen. You are going to need to change. You can change. You really will change. It's incredibly important that you do. And it is vital for this world. So it's about you.

Some of us struggle with this. Perhaps partly we have misunderstood John the Baptist's declaration: 'He must become greater – I must become less' (John 3:30). It's a statement which shows John's deep humility, and his clear understanding of his role and who Jesus was. In the right context, it is a noble and worthy prayer to offer. But some of us have applied it wholesale to ourselves and developed a sort of 'worm' theology. A theology which implies that for Jesus to increase we must become nothing.

I don't buy that.

Father God did not create you and me to become nothing. He does not regard you, in any shape or form, as nothing. He has not made a mistake with you. He wants you to look like Jesus, yes. But Jesus must increase as you *increase* – in your Jesus-ness, in your beauty, in your personality and in your co-operation with all that God has in mind for you. It's in becoming more like Jesus that the real you becomes stronger. The you that Father God carefully and wonderfully created. The true you!

The person you are and what God wants to do with you and in you – that's you, sitting in your room, or on your commute, wearing your clothes, reading this book, thinking of your day, the people you will meet, the things that you will do. Don't think someone else's room or someone else's clothes or someone else's day. Yes, you, that you – you are crucial to God's plan, the person you are and what God wants to do with you is crucial for his plan for the world. Playing small is not going to bless anyone – and ultimately it is not going to glorify him. Yes, he wants to change you. He wants to make you more like Jesus. But in doing this, he's making you more like *you*.

It is almost as if inside you there is another you. The real you, the true you, the person you were called to be and created to be is in you. And that person, although it may sound ridiculous, because your experience is not this, but that person is fearless, that person is joyful, that person is supremely loving, that person is truthful, that person is life-bringing, that person is significantly encouraging. That's who you are. That's the true you. That's who you are created to be and that's what God wants for you.

It's just that in this world we experience pain. And rejection and abandonment and violence and abuse. In this world we mess up, we sin. It all conspires to limit you, mark you, destroy you.

It's all about you. And it's all about him. It's all about him in you. So, it's worth taking some time to consider something about yourself, and where you stand.

'Therefore, there is now no condemnation for those who are in Christ Jesus, because through Christ Jesus the law of the Spirit who gives life has set you free from the law of sin and death. For what the law was powerless to do because it was weakened by the flesh, God did by sending his own Son in the likeness of sinful flesh to be a sin offering. And so he condemned sin in the flesh, in order that the righteous requirements of the law might be fully met in us, who do not live according to the flesh but according to the Spirit.'

Romans 8:1–4

Let's be honest for a minute. Don't you want to really live, I mean really live, live abundantly in that promised freedom, as Father God intended? Don't you really want to be the true you? Aren't you just about sick and tired of stumbling around in the same sin and the same character failings? Of constantly thinking, 'Why can I not deal with this?' Aren't you about sick and tired of wallowing in the same lack of self-worth which means your relationships are dysfunctional because you don't know who you are and you always find yourself in competition with other people and jealous of them? Aren't you just about sick of carrying around the same unforgiveness, the same guilt that you know has been forgiven but you carry it around with you anyway? Aren't you just a bit tired of carrying the same old competitiveness, the same tendency towards criticism and judgment, and that faith-crushing cynicism? Aren't you fed up with the same desire for stuff, of being a target for the advertisers, the ones who want to sell you the shinier thing and the faster thing? Aren't you tired of succumbing to that kind of temptation? The same addiction, the same lingering illness, the same old disability, the same fear, the same hang-ups about the past, the same draw towards the expectations of others?

These burdens pull us down. They stop us being who we were created to be. They stop you being really you and me being really me. This is not how God intends us to be. God has a different plan. God invites you and I to stand.

STANDING - OR FLYING?

At the risk of confusion, let's just for a moment mix our metaphors, let's just say we are geese or aeroplanes and talk about flying. (Stay with me.)

Planes are the most ridiculous things. Seriously. Have you ever wondered how they fly? How do A380s actually stay in the air? Think about it (you probably have). Hundreds of tons of metal, plastic, smiley air hostesses and weird little cans of coke, find themselves, somehow, effortlessly soaring across the vast skies. How do they stay up in the air? Why do these aeroplanes fly?

The answer is simple – it's because of a higher law, the law of aerodynamics, which is, in effect, the law of lift. They fly because that's the way they were designed. Their huge engines put them in a position, a posture to fly. In the air, planes are exactly where they are meant to be. It takes the skill of the pilot to actually force a plane down to earth again. Once it's on the ground, the engines stop, and the wings no longer channel the air to keep it aloft.

On the ground? That's a different matter. Gravity keeps the plane on the ground.

In Romans 8, Paul talks about life, and why a life lived with Jesus, a Christian life, is so extraordinary. He speaks of two laws: the law of the Spirit of life, and the law of sin and death. The law of sin and death drags us down, literally. It's like gravity. It pulls us down and keeps us earthbound. But there is a higher law: the law of lift. Sin is just like the gravity that keeps the plane grounded. However, in Christ, we are subject to a higher law: the law of lift, the law of the Spirit of life.

We need the law of the Spirit of life. We need to operate in it, under it, and through it. The law of gravity runs deep in us and our default position would be grounded if it weren't for this wonderful grace. This law of the Spirit of life equips us to fly. Again, it's the way we are designed. It's everything our designer intends us to be.

TRUE YOU | 11

I think we can extend Paul's analysis, as we often seem to live under a third law. We might call it 'the law of taxiing'. It could also be called 'the law of potential', which sticks at potential and becomes 'the law of going nowhere, not very fast'. This 'law of amazing future potential' is eclipsed by our perpetual state of self-imposed grounding. The law of Woulda! Coulda! Shoulda!

It's not quite sin and death – but it's certainly not life and lift. It's clearly not the worst law to live under but it's certainly the most frustrating. Have you ever sat on a runway waiting to take off?

A MORAL TALE

Way before aeroplanes and smiley hostesses were even thought of, Søren Kierkegaard, the Danish philosopher and theologian, wrote a story about this very thing. He called it: *The Domestic Goose: A Moral Tale*.

In his tale, a flock of geese go to church to worship each Sunday. The sermon they hear at church is the same each and every week. The minister, 'the High Goose', talks about geese and the incredible destiny that is available for each of them. He tells them that the Creator has made them for flight, and that they are called to fly to distant pastures. He informs them that this is a deeply noble calling. Every time the Creator's name is mentioned, the geese curtsy and the ganders bow and yet the High Goose's evocative rhetoric is never, ever, taken seriously. In reality the geese are so well fed and fat that they long ago lost their ability to fly. In fact, many geese believed that their plumpness was indeed the blessing of the Creator upon them. A few crazy geese attempted this thing called flight. It was tough and they were seen as well meaning, but ultimately weird and extreme. Sunday after Sunday, the geese gathered at church. They heard the same glorious sermon about destiny, about glory and about … flight. They agreed, they nodded and they said 'Amen to that!' Then they waddled home.

A flock of geese in flight is an inspiring sight. But flightless geese would be strange creatures. They'd lack purpose, grace and nobility. They'd lack the very essence that makes them geese.

Kierkegaard's story is as relevant today as it ever was. You and I were made for flight. We were made to 'soar on wings like eagles', and to know the freedom, adventure and nobility that is the mark of true humanity. And most of us, who call ourselves Christians, completely agree on that. We even say 'Amen to that!'

And then we waddle away home.

God invites us to so much more than we accept. We believe that God wants great things for us – but more often we believe that God can do that, rather than will do that. I know that this sounds a little subtle, a minor distinction, it is rather more like missing the whole point. Unless I really become who I was made to be, unless I am really free, unless I really stand, unless I fly, I become less me or not me. See it's easy to be set free and not actually be free.

FREE – OR NOT FREE

We live only two yards free – just outside the prison gates and with our back turned to a limitless horizon. We fix on not-sinning-very-much, and constantly fail in that. We know we can't do it, can't make it, can't fix it, can't run it. But we still try. We spend our entire lives attempting to drag ourselves out of sin and death and the best we manage is taxiing.

Sometimes even the cycle of our church teaching keeps us earthbound. We return to the building each week to hear eloquent sermons on human sinfulness, carefully composed to remind us of the beauty and wonder of God's grace. More often than not, they're sincerely intended to keep us near the cross. We hear wonderful truths, yet if we are not careful the cross of Jesus becomes only the destination point for our lives when it is also supposed to be the embarkation point for life, for flight, for standing.

Now, don't hear what I'm not saying. At the heart of the gospel there is a call to self-sacrifice – I do believe that. But there is *also* the promise of Jesus to life in all its fullness. Abundance. Freedom.

It is finished. We've been released. Jesus frees us.

Let that sink in. It is for freedom that Christ has set us free. And yet we hold back. Jesus came so that we might have life in all its fullness, not a contrived life suffocated by all its efforts and strife. He came to win us full forgiveness, not semi-acceptance. He came to show us grace, not legalism. He came for relationship, not religion. Jesus became man for us to know God, to stand in relationship with him, to know intimacy with him. Not for us to maintain a respectful distance.

Jesus came so you and I could stand. So you could be you. I mean really you. And because of this you can be the transformation that this world needs. As curious as this all is, it really is all about you! Your story is part of his story. Of course you were made to fly. Well not literally. But you were made to stand. To walk, to run. You were made to be you.

It's all about you. It's all about him. It's all about him in you. To change the world.

——————————— SO: ———————————

We are left with questions. Many questions. It might be good to ask ourselves some of them now. Take a quiet half hour to think about them. Find a Bible. Find a comfortable chair. Find a small mirror. Maybe a notebook and a pen.

Look in the mirror. Then ask yourself these questions. Maybe write down your answers. Be honest: this is just between you and him.

- How do you describe the person you see? Physically? Emotionally? Spiritually? Potentially?
- What are you trying to prove? To whom?
- What are you afraid of losing?
- How do you think Father God describes you?

Now. Read these passages. Slowly. Allow them to sink in. What do they say about how Father God sees you? It might help to say it aloud or write down your answer. Something like this.

Psalm 139 ... *'God knows me. I am fearfully and wonderfully made.'*
Galatians 4:9 ... *'Father God knows me.'*

Song of Songs 4:9 ...
John 3:16 ...
1 Peter 1:18–19 ...
1 Corinthians 12:27 ...
1 John 3:1–2 ...
Galatians 3:28 ...
Ephesians 1:13 ...
1 Corinthians 3:16 ...
Matthew 5:13 ...
Matthew 5:14–16 ...

Now, read on ...

2.

GROW YOUR OWN JESUS

'But what about all the miracles? The healings? Raising people from the dead? Doesn't that prove that Jesus was God? You know, more than human?'

'No, it proves that Jesus is truly human.'

'What?'

The Shack, William P Young (2007)

•

He is the image of the invisible God, the firstborn over all creation. For by him all things were created: things in heaven and on earth, visible and invisible, whether thrones or powers of rulers or authorities; all things were created by him and for him. He is before all things and in him all things hold together. And he is the head of the body, the church. He is the beginning and the firstborn from among the dead, so that in everything he might have the supremacy.

Colossians 1:15–18

A family friend came back from a trip to the USA and brought us a present. It was a 'Grow Your Own Jesus'. Awesome! The idea is that you stick him in a glass of water and overnight he grows to about six times his original size. We thought it was a fun present and we rushed down each morning to see how big Jesus was. And indeed our Jesus grew. Then he shrank again. Jesus made us laugh.

You should get one.

Maybe you already have one? Many of us do. We do try to grow our own Jesuses. We take an idea of Jesus and try to conform, or reform it, into an image that we are comfortable with. The kind of image that suits us. Maybe we like the idea of 'Soft Jesus', so we feminise him, or camp him up, and keep him on a shelf in the kitchen. Or maybe we prefer the other extreme and pump him up to be 'Cage Fighter Jesus'.

But Jesus is not a sponge. Or a fluffy toy. He may not even have a six pack. Jesus *is*. He simply is. He is who he is. In his own words, he is the *I AM*.

Jesus. Do you know him? The real Jesus? Truly?

Sometimes I ask myself. I've spent half a lifetime and a career and so much energy ... actually I am a professional in introducing people to Jesus. But do I have Jesus down? Can you ever? Or is that the problem? Take a minute to think about it.

How do you see Jesus? Friend, brother, lord, saviour, king, priest, God? What is your picture of Jesus?

I asked myself that question. It seemed only fair, if I was to ask you, that I try and answer it first. I found it hard. My response was confusing.

See Jesus is my friend and companion – but he also happens to be the King of Kings and the Lord of Lords. He comforts me and disturbs me in equal measure. He makes me uncomfortably comfortable and leaves me feeling secure and expectant. He gives me rest and keeps me on my toes. I love that he is the Lion of the Tribe of Judah and that he has all power for me. I love that he is the Lamb of God who was slain for me. To me he is extreme power and extreme grace and everything in between. He is everything. Without him I am nothing. With him suddenly all things are possible. I love that he takes hold of me and I reach out to take hold of him. Sometimes I catch him. But there is always more. And it is always disturbing comfort. It is intimacy and awe.

But I have always struggled with the 'Jesus is my boyfriend' idea. I hate worship songs that encourage me to think that he's somehow my lover. If that's your bag, that's fine, but it doesn't work for me. For me, Jesus is my older brother, the one who has gone before me, the one who paves the way for me, the one who sticks up for me. He is the adventurer, leader, and the one who calls me on and calls me up and draws me in. He protects me. He gives me confidence. Perhaps because I never had an older brother – I had to pave the way myself. But Jesus has my back, he's at my right hand, he's my authority, my card of reference. He's the one who calls me to battle, and fights on my behalf. He's the one who calls me to rest, and gives me confidence to do so. When I don't know the way to turn, he's there. When I've never been this way before, he has.

In all the training I've done, I'm not sure that anyone ever taught me about the person of Jesus. I studied a number of views and pictures of Jesus, but either I was never taught well or I never engaged properly with the importance of who I understood Jesus to be. And that's crucial.

Because if Jesus is supposed to grow in you, you'd better work out what that looks like.

You can know as much as you like but you'll never completely know Jesus, you'll never come to the end of knowing Jesus, of what there is to know and ways of knowing him. It's all about Jesus. The vision is Jesus, the strategic plan is Jesus, the origin is Jesus, the goal is Jesus.

So. Luke 4. New Testament Nazareth. Jesus was home for the weekend. He went to the synagogue. And when he stood up to read, 'All spoke well of him and the gracious words that came from his lips.' 'Isn't this Joseph's son?' (You can almost hear them saying 'How he's grown!') But instead of accepting their faintly patronising praise, instead of allowing small-town Nazareth to own him, Jesus speaks out. He challenges them, he tells them what they are really thinking. He infuriates them to the extent that they want to kill him.

Think about it. In the course of a short sermon Jesus' own childhood neighbours and friends turn from loving his gracious words to physically trying to kill him. That must have been some sermon.

Jesus always, always provokes a reaction. Throughout the gospels, people are astonished, amazed, they fall down at his feet, they run from his whip, they climb trees to catch a glimpse of him, they gnash their teeth at him, they give up everything to follow him. Which, if you think about it for just a minute, is hard to imagine happening today, even in the most happening of high streets, even to the most popular of celebrities. And no-one, not one of them, can make Jesus do what they want him to do, or be what they want him to be.

Jesus is who he is.

Jesus is who he is in all his authority and in all his foot-washing servanthood and in all his sacrifice and in all his submission and in all his righteous anger. We can't tame him, we can't domesticate him, and we shouldn't diminish or emasculate him.

We can only *try* to know him. To become like little children and somehow or other get our minds and our hearts and our souls around who he might possibly be. To allow him to disturb us. To unsettle us. To stir us with his love, his grace, his compassion, his forgiveness and his truth. To allow him to know us. And to grow in us.

Jesus is. And he *is* in you. And me. And he needs to grow. You don't get to grow your own Jesus. He, the real Jesus, needs to grow in you.

The real Jesus.

JESUS EXPOSED

So Jesus shows up on our planet. Walking and talking and loving and healing. And telling stories. And he himself walks into a story that started with creation and isn't finished yet. It's a familiar story, one that the crowd knew very well, but let me remind us ...

- First, there's the story of *Creation*. God said 'Let there be light' and there was light, and God saw that the light was good. A story that defined purpose. In a garden. In this world. A story that spoke of roles and identity and work and family and love and creativity.
- Next up, the *Exodus* story. Egypt and plagues and God's call to 'Let my people go'. Splitting seas and manna and quails. A story of rebellion, a story of a journey, a story of freedom.
- And then, *Exile*. By the rivers of Babylon we sat and wept when we remembered Zion. A story of return and restoration. The return to a promised land. The return to relationship.
- Finally, the *Priestly* story. A story that tries to make sense of lambs under arms, queues in Jerusalem and blood, lots of blood. A story of sacrifices and atonement, pigeons and doves. The brokering of a transaction. The desperate wait for the Messiah.

This is the context, these are the stories. Stories pregnant with expectation, brimming full of hope. The prophets say he's coming. The people hope he's coming. At last, the wild man of the desert cries, 'He's come. He is among us!' And like an unpinned hand grenade, Jesus hurls himself, exploding into this world of stories, this world of law and of prophecies. And he says, 'It's all about me. Everything has been heading towards me, all the stories of our world, the creation story, the exile story and the returning, the priestly story and all the blood and sacrifice – it's all about me. I am the Creator and Sustainer. I am the Redeemer. I am the Restorer. I am the Saviour of the world. I didn't come to destroy these stories. I came to fulfil these stories. It's all about me.'

He's not abolishing the law, he's not contradicting the prophets. He's fulfilling them.

Jesus makes sense of the stories that have come before. Stories that find their conclusion, their meaning, and their validity in him. It was through him that all things were created, so he calms storms with a word and feeds thousands on a boy's fish supper. He stamps on the serpent's head at the gates of Eden as he straightens the back of a doubled up daughter of Abraham. The blood daubed on the doorposts is his, freedom from slavery is from him. The stories all point to him, they are all about him.

It is all about him.

HIS NAME IS…

This Jesus has many names. And his names are remarkable.

He is called the Christ, which means 'the anointed one of God'. In prophetic writings he is named Wonderful Counsellor, Mighty God, Everlasting Father and Prince of Peace. He's described as the Lily of the Valley and the Bright Morning Star. He is beautiful. He is said to be the Lion of the Tribe of Judah and at the same time the Lamb of God who takes away the sin of the world. In other words he can do absolutely anything because he has all power and what he has chosen to do is to take his supreme competence and give his life. He is everything.

Jesus is the Bread of Life and the one who gives us living water. He is the Great Physician. The blind see, the lame walk, the deaf hear, the dead are raised. He is the Good Shepherd and the Friend of Sinners. He is the Lord and we worship him. He is the Bridegroom and we wait for him. He is the Master and he calls us friends.

Jesus describes himself as the Alpha and the Omega. The first and the last, the beginning and the end. He is the capstone, the gate, the doorway, he is what it is all founded on, and the entrance to life.

One of my favourite descriptions of Jesus comes from Paul. Paul says Jesus is the image of the invisible God. He is the likeness, the manifestation of the God that previously could not be seen. He is the firstborn, the owner, the ranking one. He is creator of all things, of humming birds and wild orchids, of snow leopards and Hebridean sunsets. And of human beings, conceived in Jesus' head and heart and created by the word of his mouth. He created the universe and holds it, so if he takes his finger off the pulse it collapses, implodes, ceases to be. Because in him all things hold together. And Jesus is the head of the church – get this – the church, my church, your church – in *everything* he has the supremacy. (Colossians 1:15–18)

When Paul says 'over everything' he's not messing around. Try, just for a moment, to get your head around what it means to be head over all things. It means that he is authoritative and has conscious active rule over all history, all human beings, all demonic powers, all disease, all disability, all nature, whether hurricanes, volcanoes, flooding, earthquakes, global warming, all businesses, all credit crunches, all healthcare, all avian flu, all sports, all elections, all computers, all military might, all governments, all religions, all culture – we only get to create culture because we are the King's kids – all universities, all stars, all galaxies, all molecules, all atoms, all atomic particles and ten thousand things no man or woman has yet discovered. Right now. Jesus rules over everything. Conscious, active, authoritative rulership.

And this is the Jesus who lives in us. The very same. The very same who needs to grow in us. Being one with Jesus is going to change everything.

Jesus in you is going to change everything. If you let him. Stop for a moment and take that in.

You are in Christ.

BE ME

Since, then you have been raised with Christ, set your hearts on things above, where Christ is, seated at the right hand of God. Set your minds on things above, not on earthly things. For you died, and your life is now hidden with Christ in God. When Christ, who is your life, appears, then you also will appear with him in glory.

Colossians 3:1–4

This intriguing verse amplifies Jesus' commission in John 20. There, Jesus passes his mandate to his disciples and says 'As the Father has sent me, I am sending you' (John 20:21). He breathes on them and they receive the Holy Spirit. He gives to them his authority. Same calling, same anointing, same style, same authority. Same Spirit. Jesus is saying to the disciples *Go, and be me.* Your life is now hidden with Christ in God!

He says the same to us today. We are disciples. We get to carry God's Great Story on. This is huge. The potential and opportunity is massive!

Very truly I tell you, whoever believes in me will do the works I have been doing, and they will do even greater things than these, because I am going to the Father.

John 14:12

Can we really do things that are even greater than Jesus did on earth? Jesus says we can.

You may be thinking, 'Jesus is God, I am not. How can I be like him? I can only hope to try to be like him.' There is no denying the divinity of Jesus. He was fully God and he was fully man. He didn't come with armies and fanfares as the Jews longed he would. Jesus chose to operate out of a veiled divinity. Jesus,

Who, being in very nature God,
did not consider equality with God something to be grasped

but he made himself nothing,
taking the very nature of a servant.

Philippians 2:6, 7 (NIV 1984)

Jesus *chose* to operate on earth primarily out of his humanity. When he healed people, and when he dealt with the demonic, he did so as a human. He knew the key to spiritual power. He knew it was listening to the Father, submitting to the Father's voice and heart, and doing so in the power of the Holy Spirit.

Jesus clearly submits to the Father: 'For I did not speak of my own accord, but the Father who sent me commanded me what to say and how to say it' (John 12:49). And Jesus operates in the power of the Spirit: '"The Spirit of the Lord is on me, because he has anointed me"' (Luke 4:18).

Listen, we are not being called to an impossible task. We are being invited into a deeper unity with Jesus. We are asked only to operate as he did in submission to Father God, and in the power of the Holy Spirit. Being one with Jesus doesn't simply mean that we share in his glory and his suffering. It means we share all the beauty of his complete humanity.

Those of us who have trusted Jesus and follow him have almost certainly resolved in our minds any intellectual or theological debates about his divinity. Perhaps however we have not fully engaged with, or squared in our thinking, the truth and implications and consequences of him being human. It might even be that this is one of the most significant issues of our age.

TAKING YOUR CALLING A LITTLE DEEPER

The New Testament shows Jesus as human in his actions, in his emotions and in his needs. He was hungry, he became tired, he wept. But it goes deeper than that. His humanity is our humanity – exactly the same.

Jesus is not pretending to be human any more than he is pretending to be God. 'The Word became flesh and made his dwelling among us' (John 1:14). The use of the word 'became' is highly significant. And, 'it was necessary for him to be made in every respect like us, his brothers and sisters' (Hebrews 2:17 NLT).

In experiencing humanity and temptation, every bit as real as ours, Jesus lived totally and consistently in obedience to the Father and in the power of the Spirit. He was 'tempted in every way, just as we are – yet was without sin' (Hebrews 4:15). He modelled true humanity. Humanity as God intends us to be in the here and now.

We assume we know what it is like to be human: its limitations, its failings. And yet, as the Nicene Creed puts it, the only Son of God 'became incarnate ... and was made man'. So Jesus defines what true humanity was and is intended to be.

'Apart from Christ we know neither what our life, nor our death is; we do not know what God is, nor what we ourselves are.' Blaise Pascal (Pensees 7).

Jesus is supposed to grow in you – his power, his character, his nature his style. Simple – but not simple.

GROWING THE JESUS IN YOU

So what does it look like, this Jesus life, this Jesus stand?

Well, different. See, Jesus' way is different, opposite, *counter* to our way. His way is counter cultural and it has become counter intuitive. In his economy, everything appears upside down. In reality it is right side up. Our experience tells us that his way is difficult, road-blocked, gridlocked and impassable, impossible. Everything appears to militate against our ability to become truly like him. To become truly ourselves.

But. Jesus beckons us on. Through. Up. Over.

Matthew 5. Jesus sits down on a hillside and starts to talk about his kingdom. He describes what it looks like to follow him. And what he says turns everything on its head.

'Blessed are the poor in spirit, for theirs is the kingdom of heaven'

Those listening to Jesus are farmers and fishermen, free men and slaves. They are dependent, they depend on the weather, on the political climate, on their bodies staying healthy, on each other, on God. They can't rely on themselves.

Our culture is about self. It is built on self-help and self-reliance. We applaud self-made men and women. We worship competence and independence. We believe we can do it on our own. Without help from others. Without help from God. Without Jesus. Yet we have been programmed for dependence. We are designed to rely on God and worship him. So: blessed are the reliant and the dependent. Blessed are those who know they need God, who depend on him, every day and every hour. Blessed are the poor in spirit.

What will it look like as Jesus grows in us? As we stand in him? We will rely on God more and more. And he is reliable, he is dependable and all the resources of heaven will be ours.

'Blessed are those who mourn, for they will be comforted'

Jesus mourns over those who are far from God, just as he wept over Jerusalem and longed to gather her to him 'as a hen gathers her chicks under her wings' (Luke 13:34).

As Jesus grows in us, our hearts will break for the lost, for the things that break the Father's heart. When we are far from Jesus it is easy to put things out of our minds, and not let them affect us. And yet when we come to Jesus he gives us a new heart, a heart of flesh, which mourns. As Jesus grows in us, we will mourn. Over poverty, injustice, abuse, families ripped apart, war and inequality. Our hearts will break over the sin in our lives – sin that distances us from the God who loves us. And as we mourn we will know the comfort of the Father.

'Blessed are the meek, for they will inherit the earth'

Bizarre. Those who don't want to inherit the earth get it all. This is genius. It flies in the face of the prevailing wind of our culture. Our world says: 'Look out for number one', and then we do. Our world says: 'We have rights', and so we want them. But we don't want responsibilities. Our world says: 'Blessed are the social climbers, the go-getters, the conquerors', but somehow it doesn't work. It's never enough. Our world cannot satisfy us.

As Jesus grows in us we will become meek – not so much a Moses-sandaled meekness, but something inherently powerful, something brought utterly under control. A wild stallion broken in.

It is not a passive meekness. It is not a kind of niceness, not about not wanting to be any trouble to anyone, not about apologising for being there or being happy with whatever anyone else wants. It's not a British middle-class meekness. Jesus' example was not a weak meekness – he constantly confronted the religious leaders, flouting their religious laws and turning over tables. There are things we can stand up to and say no to. But Jesus also consistently talks about selling all you have, giving to the poor, turning the other cheek, losing your life to find it. And his example is obedience unto death.

No, this meekness is an active laying down of our lives, a relentless reaching out for God, and not settling for anything less. This meekness is something strong and powerful. When Jesus grows in you, you will stand strong.

'Blessed are those who hunger and thirst for righteousness, for they will be filled'

We often settle for the wrong things. Like fast food – preferably high in fat and ladled with sugar. It's convenient and tastes good. And yet it never satisfies. It invariably leaves you with a fatty aftertaste and still hungry. It is the same in the rest of life: we settle for the quick fix, the easy solution, and the compromise, which gets us by. But we ache for something more.

Deep down, you hunger for right, and so do I. And we know that Jesus is right, that Jesus in you is predisposed to provoke right-ness, righteousness. But what does that mean, this word 'righteousness'? What does it mean to 'seek first the kingdom of God and his righteousness' (Matthew 6:33, ESV)? What does it look like?

A better translation could be 'seek first the kingship of Jesus and his restorative justice'. Righteousness is not first about the morality of your heart and your actions. It is first about your participation in the Father's restoration plan, which will then, in his time and in his way, result in a changed heart and changed action.

Maybe it means what we sometimes call 'making a difference'. Maybe it is something to do with 'doing the right thing', or 'not looking the other way', or 'living worthwhile lives'. Maybe it was something of Jesus' righteousness that provoked William Booth to pour his life out working to support the urban poor. Perhaps it was righteousness that provoked Jackie Pullinger to pour hers out in Hong Kong helping the addicts in the Walled City there. Maybe it provoked Cathy to leave her job as a high powered IT consultant for Heineken and establish a business teaching homeless people a skill and a living, baking cakes for local establishments and selling them. Maybe it provokes you to do something. I don't know.

What I do know for certain is that as Jesus grows in us, he makes us hungry, but not hungry for junk. We will hunger for doing the right thing, for his restorative justice, for making a difference. And, as Jesus grows in us, we will be filled. Our junk is replaced, again and again, with his *right-ness*, with his righteousness.

'Blessed are the merciful, for they will be shown mercy'

Mercy is at the core, in the very DNA of the Godhead. The Godhead is merciful and operates out of mercy, on our behalf. So, as we pursue Jesus and oneness with him, we too will increasingly operate out of mercy. We will love forgiveness and we will delight in giving others the grace that they do not deserve.

We will no longer look out for number one, because we will prefer to make everyone else number one. We fill find contentment in the second seat. We will find ourselves drawn to those who have not, and to those who are hopeless. And God loves it!

'Blessed are the pure in heart, for they will see God'

Our hearts can be drawn to so many things. We love new, shiny stuff, and our magazines and screens are filled with beautiful people. Designer accessories carried by the carefully designed. But it is superficial. Our society is obsessed with what's on the outside. It infests our culture and it gets hold of our hearts like a parasite. We are captured by what we see. We judge on appearances. We become distracted by and obsessed with what we look like, what we have, what's on the surface, when God cares so much more for what's below – what's *in*.

The love of stuff – shiny stuff, new stuff, stuff to make me look good – is not the Jesus way. It will not make our hearts clean and shiny and new. It will tarnish and pollute them. And it will never satisfy.

As you stand close to Jesus, as Jesus grows in you, so does truth and loyalty, purity of speech, honesty and integrity, righteousness. It becomes natural. At the same time, as Jesus grows in you, it becomes hard for lies to live with you, for disloyalty to be part of you, for dishonesty to have any part in your life.

This is the outward working, the visual expression of the inner holiness that is about proximity to Jesus. This is what it looks like for Jesus to grow in you.

The Jesus kingdom goes so much deeper. Here, it is not clean hands that Jesus pronounces as blessed, but a pure heart. It's truly rich and you'll want more and more of it. And you can have more and more of it!

And those who seek to go deeper with God will be purified inside and out. They will see God. They will actually see God: see his face, the reward of prophets, like Moses and Elijah. When Moses came out from meeting God his face was radiant, literally shining (Exodus 34:29)! How much cooler than all our shiny stuff will that be!

'Blessed are the peacemakers, for they will be called sons of God'

God is a peacemaker. He is not a warmonger. He is involved. And Jesus is the Prince of Peace. Jesus calls us to get involved. To mediate. To reconcile.

'Blessed are those who are persecuted because of righteousness, for theirs is the kingdom of heaven'

Sometimes, as Jesus grows in us, and we start to act in the right way, it shows. It stands out. Sometimes he actually asks us to stand out, to stand up for what is right. It might be supporting a colleague at work who is being given a hard time, or refusing to go along with a lie. It is rarely popular and never easy. It might cost us popularity, or promotion. It might cost us our job. And we might not get it back, not in this lifetime. But we gain the kingdom of heaven itself.

People persecute those who are different. Perhaps some of the time we are not different enough – not meek enough, not passionate enough, not loving enough, not one with Christ enough – to be worth persecuting just yet. But we could be.

Bring on difference.

Bring on persecution.

Bring on unity.

• • •

I have three brothers. Reuben, Alex and James.

James loves action, speed and adventure. He loves to wind me up and he loves his motorbike. It's a big motorbike.

James shows up at my house and offers to take me for a ride – just for a bit. After a mile or so, I'm scared. Really scared. But you don't tell your younger brother you're scared. We've nearly come off more than once. Each corner I sit upright, poker straight, rigid as a board. But James is cool. James is calm. James is completely in control. At the first set of lights he turns to me and says firmly, 'When I lean – you lean!'

I learn to lean. I learn to trust. It's an incredible ride.

Allow Jesus to grow in you. His power, his adventure, his humility, his style, his kingdom. Jesus on the front – you on the back. Complete co-operation. He leans, you lean.

―――――――――――――― SO: ――――――――――――――

Jesus is the first disciple. Ever thought about that? It's not just that I am his disciple but he is the model, examplar disciple. I am invited to walk in his shadow to represent with ever increasing skill his commission and his likeness.

Why don't you commit yourself to re-reading one of the gospels? (I know you have read them before and think you know them pretty well, but humour me!) This time read it through the filter of 'That's how I'm supposed to live, that's what I'm supposed to do, that's who I'm supposed to be.'

As you read about Jesus, watch and see what he does, listen to his words and hear him. Ask yourself how this translates into your world, your life, your encounters today and tomorrow and this week.

You might also like to read:

The Jesus I never knew, Philip Yancey (Zondervan 1995)

The Gospel according to Jesus, Chris Seay (Thomas Nelson 2010)

PART 2.

STAND UP AND STAND FOR

•

Who are you to judge someone else's servant? To their own master, servants stand or fall. And they will stand, for the Lord is able to make them stand.

Romans 14:4

STAND UP. DON'T SIT BACK. DON'T JUST SIT THERE. STAND UP. ACT. DO SOMETHING.

EASY TO SAY. HARDER TO DO.

THAT WHICH IS HARD BECOMES THAT WHICH IS IMPOSSIBLE WHEN THERE IS INSECURITY AROUND IDENTITY AND UNCERTAINTY ABOUT PURPOSE.

STAND UP. THIS IS WHO YOU ARE.

STAND FOR. THIS IS WHAT YOU ARE ABOUT.

3.

MY NAME IS SON

SOMETHING ABOUT IDENTITY

I believe that what we become depends on what our fathers teach us at odd moments, when they aren't trying to teach us. We are formed by little scraps of wisdom.

Foucault's Pendulum, Umberto Eco (1988)

•

'I always wondered why God was supposed to be a father', she whispers. 'Fathers always want you to measure up to something. Mothers are the ones who love you unconditionally, don't you think?'

Keeping Faith, Jodi Picoult (1999)

•

See what great love the Father has lavished on us, that we should be called children of God! And that is what we are! The reason the world does not know us is that it did not know him.

1 John 3:1

I used to live next to a really lovely family. Three kids. The youngest daughter was beautiful. She was very intelligent and had an attractive personality. She also loathed herself. Most of all, she loathed the way she looked. Physically, she was tiny, but her mind told her she was fat. And so, she starved herself. She became a waif and then she became a ghost. It broke her family's hearts. And no one could understand it.

You may have stories like this. Of people who don't know how much they are loved, don't know who they are. They are many. Because ours is a culture in crisis. We are a people who don't know who we are. This goes deeper than not knowing what we look like, than not seeing how others see us. It is a deep spiritual identity crisis. We are immersed in deep loss.

We are living with the consequences of a cosmic case of identity theft. Stolen in the garden, and pilfered through the generations.

It's not how it has to be. It's not how it should be. We don't need to identify ourselves by what we work as, what we drive, or what size we wear. We needn't be labelled by letters after names, schools attended, or positions held in church.

We have to see each other, and importantly, ourselves, as we are meant to be seen. We need to fully understand who we are in Christ. His sacrifice bought more than salvation. It bought emancipation from the need to bow to these cancerous self-image measures and markers. It bought the privilege of confidence in who we are: finely honed creations of the magnificent living God. It bought us the privilege of becoming sons of God.

STICKS AND STONES

Somewhere along the track we all got named. And it didn't happen just once. For most of us, we got called something on the day we were born. I was called Karl Andrew, but to my mother, I was 'Kandy'. Fortunately it never stuck. But it doesn't end with the names our parents give us. We get named and renamed again, and again and again.

We take these new names – some are given, and some are thrown. They are often less than flattering. We're called something, described as something, maybe 'fat', or 'stupid', or worse. Sometimes we ache from them. Sometimes we act from them. Sometimes we take phrases as names:

'You'll always let us down!'
'You're just like your dad!'

And usually such names mean separation and isolation.

'This school's not for the likes of you.'

You can probably still hear the rest. We were given labels. We got named.

A friend, Paul Scanlon, helped me with this. He used to say that both John the Baptist and Jesus were given to earthly parents. They were entrusted to their care. God trusted two humble, Middle Eastern couples to bring up two very special boys. One was a prophet. The other the Son of Man himself. But there was something God did not allow the earthly parents to do. They were not permitted to name their boys. Father God named them: '"you are to call him John"' (Luke 1:13); '"you are to call him Jesus"' (Luke 1:31).

Get this. Only God has the right to truly name you.

Think about this. Think of your first name, and even your surname. So familiar. So much part of your identity. Could it be that these are not your true names? They are certainly not your full name. Your full name, your real name, always ends with 'son/daughter of God'. Your identity starts with this, the name that God calls you. And who God calls you to be starts in the context of his fatherhood. And one of the names he calls you, is 'Son'.

NUTELLA LOVE

The apostle John talks about the father: 'See what great love the Father has lavished on us, that we should be called children of God! And that is what we are!' (1 John 3:1)

That word 'lavished'. It's carefully chosen. It suggests a vast love, poured out for us, and spread over us. Think hazelnut chocolate spread on warm toast. I think that if the apostle John was editing this version of the Bible there would be triple exclamation marks, it would be bold, underlined and italicised. We are not to miss this: 'that we should be called children of God!'

Sons of God! A son is a son. Not an acquaintance. Not an onlooker or bystander. Not friend or colleague. Not slave. Not employee or servant or secretary or assistant. A son.

Of course he does also call some of us 'daughter'. But stay for a moment with son, because he would call all of us 'son'. Even if we might happen to be a girl. There's no ambiguity here. That's our identity, and everything else about us stems from that status – from that gift of fatherhood, from a God who lavishes his love on us. A God who loves us to call him, 'our Father'.

This is the God who says you are 'fearfully and wonderfully made' (Psalm 139:14). This is the God who 'saw your unformed body' and declared it good (Genesis 1:31). See? God is your Dad.

GIRLS TOO

You are a son of God. A son of God! Now I know that's hard to get your head around – especially if you're a girl – but stay with me.

It is not being exclusive, or sexist, to suggest that all of us, irrespective of gender, race, socio-economic status, sexual orientation, or any other divider we tend to use – *all* of us – get to be sons of God. This is important. Inheritance in Jesus' day tended to be patrilineal. It was passed from father to son.

Of course this seems to suck if you are a daughter – but remember that in the kingdom of God all daughters are also sons. And all the sons who happen to be male, well they have their own gender mind bender! Sons have to deal with being the bride of Christ later in our story.

We are sons.
We are the Bride.
Gender is not the primary issue

I hope I would be the first to admit that the church has a pretty deplorable record when it comes to the way in which it has treated women down through the years. I do all I can to help women find and develop their gifts and use them to glorify God.

So in that context, hear me. We have to let go of our life-choking political correctness just long enough to grasp this wonderful truth, that – regardless of your gender:

You are a son of God!

Jesus knew who he was. He was a son, *the* Son of God. In his earthly existence he operates as a son. It's his primary identity.

The Father treats Jesus as his son. When Jesus is baptised into his ministry, his Father is there watching, and he speaks like a father to his son: "You are my son, whom I love; with you I am well pleased" (Mark 1:11) and he speaks his love *over* him, so all can hear, affirming Jesus before the crowd. Another day up on a mountaintop he speaks out of a cloud "This is my Son, whom I love; with him I am well pleased. Listen to him!" (Matthew 17:5) Like a father, he loves the Son and he tells him he loves him. He shows him what he is doing, he teaches him, he trusts him with responsibility, he wants him to be honoured, he testifies in his favour, he is with him (John 5:19–30; 8:28, 29).

Jesus acts like a son to his Father, imitating his Father and learning from him, working as his Father is working, doing what he sees his Father doing, speaking what his Father has taught him to say. He trusts his Father, he knows that his Father loves him and tells everyone; he knows that he has not left him alone. He loves his Father, he does what pleases his Father, talks to his Father like a son talks to his Father and he spends time with him.

And Jesus calls God 'Father'. That is the name Jesus uses for God. In fact, God is called Father just short of 200 times in the New Testament.

This may not sound like news. You may have heard this time and time again. You may be thinking, 'OK, I get it. Tell me something I don't already know, Karl.' But I need you to pause for a moment. I need you to consider this carefully.

Jesus' relationship with his Father is the primary relationship of his earthly life and a fundamental tenet of his teaching in ministry.

CALL ME 'DAD'

If you were a first century Jewish boy listening to Jesus teaching this stuff, this would have exploded your preconceptions, your whole world. That he can just show up and start talking about the Almighty as 'Dad'.

When Jesus is doing his big talk (you'll find it in Matthew 6) and he starts talking about prayer he tells us to call God '*Abba*'. (Matthew 6:9) And we roughly translate that 'Father'. But that is a really limited translation. *Abba* is an Aramaic word and the best translation is probably 'Dad' or 'Daddy' or 'Papa'. It's not formal – it's intimate. It's the kind of word you use when you have a close relationship, when you are young. It's loving. It's trusting. It's dependent. So Jesus is saying, when you talk to your Father in heaven, the Creator of the universe, call him 'Dad'.

This is mind-blowing stuff for this Jewish guy who is listening to Jesus.

Because he's learnt that this God is all-powerful. That he's the living God, he's the 'I Am', and his name is so holy it can barely be spoken. He's learnt that this God is the Unchangeable, he's the Rock, he's *Jehovah Hasour*. He's learnt that this God is the Almighty, and all-sufficient, nourisher and provider: he's *El Shaddai* who appeared to Abram and told him to walk before him and be blameless, who appeared to Jacob after he fled from his brother and gave him the name Israel. He knows that he's *Jehovah Saboath,* the Lord of the angel armies, who appeared to Isaiah so that he cried, "Woe to me, I am ruined!" (Isaiah 6:5).

And if he's been at all trained and understands any of the Scriptures, he also understands that this God is somehow involved, that he's *Jehovah Raphe,* the God who heals, who sweetened the bitter water at Marah, and protected the Israelites from the diseases of the Egyptians. He's *Jehovah Nissi,* 'the Lord is my Banner', who David praised when he collected the gifts the people freely gave for the building of the temple. He knows that he's *Jehovah Jireh*, the Lord who provides, who provided a ram caught in a thicket and allowed Abraham to spare Isaac, he's *Jehovah Shamah*, the Lord who is there, who is present, and gave this name to Jerusalem in Ezekiel's vision.

So our Jewish friend knows that God is a mighty God, a powerful God. He knows that you've got to sacrifice to him, you've got to obey his laws. He knows that he is somehow involved, but that you can't really get very close to him.

But what he's never ever heard, what he's never been taught, is the idea that this God is intimate. That he's relational and interested. That he wants to know you. That you get to call him 'Dad'.

DAD THE RUNNER

Jesus tells a story. You probably know it well. We call it the Story of the Prodigal Son – you'll find it in Luke 15. Some prefer to call it the Story of the Prodigal God. A God who:

Loves
    Gives
        Waits
            Runs
                Kisses
                    Restores

The chief characteristic of our God – of this father, this Daddy God – the thing that you would pick out is that he loves us. Weirdly, you and I are predisposed to run away from this love. There is something in our nature that is predisposed to do it our way. We're off.

And his love lets us go. God is not a bully. He's not going to force us into a relationship. As you run away from God, you run away from all his love and all his goodness – your life is going to begin to unravel. If you are living outside of the love of a wise father you're going to do stupid stuff. The Father lets it happen. Why? Because he knows that you and I need to learn that the only place we will know love and wisdom and happiness is the Father's house.

The crowds knew a story very similar to this story. But in that story the father said 'you made your bed. Now lie in it. You made your choice'. Jesus turns the story completely around. The father runs. He hitches up his skirt, and in an undignified manner, runs towards his son. He runs and he lavishes his son with kisses. His love is restorative and abundant. He takes a robe and puts it on his son's shoulders, covering his shame. He calls for sandals and a ring, restoring position and status.

You are a son of God. We are sons of God. He loves us because he loves us because he loves us. Let's have a party! Here comes life in all its fullness in the Father's house.

Perhaps we are that younger brother. We ran away. And it's time to come home.

Or perhaps we are thanking God that we are *not* the younger brother. Our feet are in the Father's house – we are clearly sons – but our experience is that we are orphans. We live a life of frustration. We miss what is right underneath our nose. Older brothers can be superior, quick to give their opinion and judgment, aware of duty. The older brother sees himself as serving the father, like a slave. That is not the way the Father wants his children to relate to him.

Both are lost. One is lost by breaking all the moral laws and doing it 'my way'. The other is lost by keeping all the moral laws and doing it 'my way'.

THE ORPHANAGE

For you did not receive a spirit that makes you a slave again to fear – but you received the Spirit of sonship. And by him we cry 'Abba, Father'.

Romans 8:15 (NIV 1984)

You're a son of God. You get to relate to God out of love and not out of fear. You have no need to serve God out of duty – you get to serve him out of joy.

So many believers are 'positional' sons, but 'experiential' orphans. We know who we are, but we don't stand in the intimacy and potential of that relationship with God. Too often we choose to live without protection, position, or security. Orphans.

My own experience of living with an orphan spirit is one of striving for recognition. Competing for affection. Attempting to earn love. It's one of defending myself – always trying to prove something. The fruit of this condition is competition, jealousy, opinion and criticism. It's not pretty – it is pretty destructive. I have lived it. And so have many of you. The root cause is not knowing God as our Father.

Listen … none of our dads, however good they were, were ever going to win the 'Dad of the Year' competition. What I am about to teach can be painful and difficult, and I wouldn't bother with it if it didn't also have the capacity to free you to be you and to stand. Your ability (and mine) to experience God as a Father who loves us unconditionally is often directly dependent on the way in which we have been fathered. Your negative experience of your Dad has the potential to damage your relationship with your heavenly Dad. Your negative experience of the people that parented you and input into your life has the potential to damage the way that you see your heavenly Father and how you operate as a son. Because often we view our heavenly Dad through the lenses of our earthly dads.

Recently, my father died. When these things happen it makes you reflect. My dad was great. I'm not sure I ever quite realised that until he'd gone. He was loud and larger than life and highly embarrassing. He loved God, life, people and me. He wasn't afraid to hug me, encourage me or tell me he loved me. He had so many qualities. But I've still had to work some things through – because he wasn't Perfect Dad. There were things I needed that he couldn't give me, and the way that I was fathered was not perfect.

As a father myself, I know – and my daughters would be the first to tell you this – that there are a whole bunch of things that I get wrong. I don't reflect perfectly the image of our heavenly Father to my kids. It's not for want of trying, it's because I'm sinful and messed up. The ways in which we've been parented by our mothers and our fathers can do damage. Here's the thing you need to understand: there is a tendency in human nature to do what was done to us. So hurt people, hurt people. If we don't deal with this we will pass it on to our children.

So. It could be your mother, your upbringing, but it's probably your father. Don't underestimate how important your dads are in the way in which they form you. They offer unconditional expressed love, they offer security, they offer praise and affirmation that all of us need in life, they offer a help in finding our purpose in life – so it may be your mum, it may be someone else, but let's take a look at Dad.

(Note: I stumbled across this teaching a few years ago and it blessed me hugely. I hope my development of it does the same for you.)

The absent father

He may have been absent because he died – or for some other reason that was not his fault. Or he may have divorced your mum or abandoned you. Or he may have been working too hard.

If that was your dad you may have a projected view of God that goes a little like this: 'If I love him, he will leave me, or he will reject me. Or he will not be there for me.' We know from the Scriptures that is not going to happen, but our experience suggests that it just might. So we have a decision to make. Are we going to trust his word or are we going to trust our experience of life? It's a huge call. It often ends up with us becoming cynical about God's word and angry about our lot.

The Bible says he is 'A father to the fatherless' (Psalm 68:5). He is God who is there. He loves to presence himself. So let him presence himself. If you have had an absent dad, God is more than capable of making up for that.

The ambivalent father

Ambivalent fathers are passive. They are not home, even when they are home. Do you know what I mean? And in the days of smart phones and tablets and constant communications, that is easy to achieve. Mum is doing the parenting, because Dad is not there, even though he's there. He may be quite shut down emotionally, he may have difficulty saying 'I love you', he may not often show physical affection. Undemonstrated love wounds, because the absence of something good hurts just as much as the presence of something bad. So if you always had to guess whether he loved you or didn't love you or was pleased with you or was not pleased with you, that is going to hurt you. The projected view of our Heavenly Father is that God may love us, but he does so from a distance. You probably think that he cannot and will not love you, so you don't really experience God, or his love in your life. You may have become someone who copes and gets by. You may have had a really hard time expressing love. And an even harder time learning how to accept love.

And here is a truth: your heavenly Father is intimately acquainted with all your ways. He is not absent, he is not passive. He wants you to know that he knows everything about you and still loves you.

The ambitious father

The ambitious father demands obedience. He has high standards. He rewards success and he punishes failure. So perhaps you were disapproved of if you didn't meet certain standards. If you came home and said 'I got 98% in my maths exam', he would say: 'What happened to the 2%?'

So now you find yourself needing to be the best. You strive for success, you think you are valued for what you do and you become great at hiding your weaknesses. Your image of God? He is interested in performance. You think 'God will reward me if I earn it'. You find yourself trying to earn love and you find yourself bound. We sometimes compound this in church. If you rest, God will judge you. If you are not running round serving like a headless chicken, then you can't actually be on fire for him.

Father God wants to release you from any expectation that is not his, and heal you. Father God is the CEO of grace – you don't have to earn it, he's just given it.

The authoritarian father

He is a legalist, not much interested in grace. He's interested in the letter of the law. He's not comfortable with love or with intimacy.

If your Dad was like that, your view of your heavenly Father is probably that God is harsh. He's not interested in your private life. Once again, out of our belief, behaviour flows. You can be pretty intolerant of anyone who doesn't think the way you think. You are good at criticism, quick to condemn people, not so good at spreading grace around. You probably don't like leadership. You probably see it as aggressive and authoritarian because that is the way you've experienced leadership before.

The abusive father

He inflicted deep emotional pain on you. The abuse may have been physical or emotional or sexual. Abuse of any kind is deeply damaging. Your experience may predispose you to struggle in seeing God as Father. If he is Father, he is a God of wrath. You see him as one to be feared and not trusted. You feel that he will hurt you if you let him close to you. You don't want to be intimate with God – in fact you can't stand the word intimate, and intimacy is something you don't want to hear about your heavenly Father.

What do we become like? Angry with God for not protecting us? We may find it really hard to draw close to God and we will find it really hard to trust other people because of the way we've been fathered.

IN THE HOUSE

Here's the truth we need to embrace: our heavenly Father is not absent, ambivalent, ambitious, authoritarian or abusive. No, he is *Abba*, he is the perfect Father. He is not the reflection of dysfunctional earthly fatherhood – he is the perfection of divine Fatherhood. He is the Daddy.

- The perfect Father loves us unconditionally. We were created with a deep need for love verbalised and acted out. He loves us, and he tells us and shows us he loves us – read 1 John 4:9.
- The perfect Father is completely dependable. He is going to let you down the twenty-second of never! His love for us and care for us does not change, ever – read James 1:17.
- The perfect Father is absolutely competent. He is *Abba* Father, and his day job is dad to you and I. But he moonlights

as Lord of the angel armies, Creator and sustainer of the universe and God Almighty, and 'nothing is impossible with God' (Luke 1:37 NIV 1984).

You are a Son of God. Your name is Son. My name is Son. This is truth! Truth to stand on. Truth to empower us to stand up and shake off our orphan clothes. Then, we will begin to live and move and minister on a completely different level. With Dad, like Dad.

Paul writes about this in Romans Chapter 8. This identity, he implies, comes with benefits.

We get power

And if the Spirit of him who raised Jesus from the dead is living in you, he who raised Christ from the dead will also give life to your mortal bodies through his Spirit, who lives in you.

Romans 8:11 (NIV 1984)

It is the very same power that raised Jesus from the dead. Power to live; power to deal with the past; power to conquer fears; power to go with the dreams God has placed in our hearts; power to be the hands and feet and mouthpiece of Jesus; power to heal and release. It's not a sinister power. It's the power of the Spirit of Jesus. Our power comes from our status, and our status comes from our Father.

You and I are powerful. Our name is Son!

We get transformation

Therefore, brothers and sisters, we have an obligation – but it is not to the flesh, to live according to it. For if you live according to the flesh, you will die; but if by the Spirit you put to death the misdeeds of the body, you will live.

Romans 8:12–13

This power will bring transformation. The inner landscape of our lives gets overhauled and we actually conform to the likeness of Jesus. This is sometimes called 'sanctification'.

With transformation comes a desire to do what is right. We are no longer subject to sin. The Spirit frees us. This transformation puts to death the junk that keeps us shackled. We have power to overcome.

God would have us come to him just as we are. We don't have to clean ourselves up or get ourselves 'right' to approach him. We just come to Abba. With our stuff, our pain, our dysfunctional families, with all our hurts. And he meets us right there. He gives us life. He affirms in us a new relationship.

Father God loves us the way we are. But he also loves us far too much to leave us the way we are.

The moment we begin to live by the Spirit, Father God begins a radical clean up and clear out of our lives. It's an upgrade that will result in freedom and glory to him.

We get guidance

Paul says sons get guidance, *'Because those who are led by the Spirit of God are sons of God'* (Romans 8:14).

He is the Spirit of truth. He is the God of Revelation. He's speaking into us all the time. Father God wants to guide his sons and daughters. That's relationship. He doesn't leave us guessing. The question we need to be constantly and naturally asking is: 'Father, what is your will?'

The fascinating truth is that when you appropriate your sonship, the clear voice of our Father drowns out the conflicting voices of our culture.

PLAYING CHURCH

Some years ago, when I was very new to being a pastor, I worked very long hours. We had four young children. Occasionally, I would come home from work to see the kids and would be greeted at the front door with:

'Daddy! Come in! We are playing Church!'

GREAT!

Some days at the moment of arriving home, I'd feel happier at the prospect of never seeing church again! That's not what I said though.

I said, 'Great! Let's play!'

I'd enter the lounge/church and be greeted at the front door by my three-year-old, who'd be handing out books, then showing me to my seat. The recorder would announce the opening song and all four girls would dutifully close their eyes. They'd wave their hands in the air and give it worship.

Next, number two daughter would take up the offering. As the only person with any money in the room/church, I'd be exhorted to give generously. (I'd never see the money again.)

Finally, at the climax of our time together in that lounge/church sanctuary, Lydia, (eldest daughter), would stand on a chair, clasping a Bible, and announce: 'I'll be Dad! I'll preach!' She'd stroke the Bible, open her mouth and, with great disdain, proclaim:

'Blah, blah, blah, blah, blah!'

Hang around *Abba* long enough and you will start looking and acting like him!

---------------------- SO: ----------------------

We need to pause here and act on some of this. Appropriating sonship may well be dependent on forgiving our fathers. You might not need to, or you might have already done this – if that is the case, please feel free to skip on to the next chapter. If not, let's pause and offer our fathers a gift they may not deserve, but which may free us to live in our sonship.

We are going to forgive our earthly dads for every way they failed to represent our heavenly Dad to us.

1. Forgive

Take some time on your own to forgive your earthly dad and to talk to your heavenly Dad. Here are some words that might help you.

Dad (substitute other authoritarian figure if necessary). *I choose to forgive you for every way that you hurt me knowingly and unknowingly. For the ways in which you misrepresented* Abba *to me. I choose to free you and release you. You owe me nothing. I actively rip up the IOU I have held in my heart. You are forgiven.*

Now heavenly Father, my true Abba, *would you perfectly father me, freeing me to be your son/daughter. Come Holy Spirit. Enable me to appropriate my sonship and walk in freedom and love.*

Now reflect for a while on what you have done. Then make sure you tell someone you trust.

2. Soak.

I'm going to challenge you to experiment with something that some of you will love and others 'not so much'. Have you ever soaked? Not in a bath or a British summer, but in the presence of God? I think soaking might really help here. Put on some gentle worship music, sit or lie down, invite the Holy Spirit to come and as you face the Father enjoy his presence. You may well find in these moments an ability to forgive others and to embrace your sonship. For some, I know, it will sound a bit weirdy. But try it anyway. Go on.

3. Reflect.

Take some time to meditate on the names of God. Look up some of these Scriptures and reflect on the contexts and stories that tell us about Father God and what he is like.

- *El Shaddai*. God the Almighty, and all sufficient. Genesis 17:1; Genesis 35:11, Exodus 6:2–3.
- *Jehovah Saboath*, the Lord of the angel armies: 1 Samuel 1:3, Psalm 24:9–10, Isaiah 6:5.
- *Jehovah Raphe*, the God who heals. Exodus 15:26, Isaiah 53:4,5.
- *Jehovah Nissi*, the Lord is my Banner. 1 Chronicles 29:11–13
- *Jehovah Jireh*, the Lord who provides. Genesis 22:14, 1 Jn 4:9. Philippians 4:19.
- *Jehovah Shamah*, the Lord who is there, who is present. Ezekiel 48:35
- *Abba*, God as Daddy, Mark 14:36, Romans 8:15, Galatians 4:6.

You might like to read:

The Father Heart of God, Floyd McClung (Harvest House Publishers 1985)

4.

GOD AT HAND

Like wind –. In it, with it, of it. Of it just like a sail, so light and strong that, even when it is bent flat, gathers all the power of the wind without hampering its course.

Like light –. In light, lit through by light, transformed into light. Like the lens which disappears in the light it focuses.

Like wind. Like light.

Just this – on these expanses, on these heights
    Markings, Dag Hammarskjöld (1964)

•

'The wind blows wherever it pleases. You hear its sound, but you cannot tell where it comes from or where it is going. So it is with everyone born of the Spirit.'
    John 3:8

Acts 1. Jesus is alive. The disciples had seen him crucified. And then they have seen him alive. They have seen him, again and again, over forty days, eating and talking and teaching them about the kingdom. He has given them 'many convincing proofs'. He is alive.

Jesus had said this is what he would do. The disciples now knew that Jesus is *exactly* who he claimed to be. The Son of God.

So, they were busting to go. Wouldn't you want the world to know? They were ready to run into their purpose, their calling, and their commission. Jesus has already said 'Go!' – 'Go into all the world and preach the gospel', 'All authority in heaven and on earth has been given to me. Therefore go and make disciples of all nations', 'As the Father has sent me, I am sending you' (Mark 16:15; Matthew 28:19; John 20:21).

And yet, now, Jesus says, 'Wait!'

Surprising? Bewildering? He says, 'Wait!' Waiting is the last thing they want to do. It just seems so ... disappointing. Why, after all that has happened, do they still have to wait?

THERE'S MORE

Well, because there is something missing. They have authority but they lack power.

They know 'the stuff', they've experienced 'the stuff' and they have been commissioned for 'the stuff', but they are not yet equipped to live 'the stuff'. So Jesus tells them to wait. He says, 'wait ... in a few days you will be baptised with the Holy Spirit ... you will receive power when the Holy Spirit comes on you' (Acts 1:4, 5, 8). *Dunamos*. Miracle power, supernatural power.

So there's a reason for the waiting: power is coming!

This power will cause them to embody, to live the truth about Jesus. This power will equip them to become witnesses to the world. That's what Jesus had asked of them and that's what Jesus had promised.

So Jesus says, 'Wait'.

And could there be something about the way he says it? A sense of expectation? There seems to be more to this act of discipline – there is anticipation. This going to blow their minds.

Incredible power is coming. Miraculous power, supernatural power, power that would make people look and wonder. Power to witness with courage and clarity, not cower and flee. Power that is convincing. Power to build community, to be church, to share all things in common. Power to lay down their lives. Power to take the gospel to the city, to the nation and to the world. Power to be who God made them to be.

Father God is giving his children power. You see, lasting transformation, real authority in ministry and witness happens not when enthusiasts whip it up, nor when it is forced out. Authentic ministry only happens as a result of the overflow of the power of God in you and I. The power of the Holy Spirit.

This power is not fleeting or limited to a few. It's for all of us. God wants to lavish his Spirit upon us. He wants to satisfy our desire for more. In every way. When Jesus says, 'But you will receive power when the Holy Spirit comes on you; and you will be my witnesses in Jerusalem, and in all Judea and Samaria, and to the ends of the earth' (Acts 1:8), that phrase 'comes on you' is the Greek preposition *epi*, 'to come upon' or 'to overflow'.

PARA, EN, EPI

It seems to me that there is a three-fold relationship between the Holy Spirit and us. It is described by three Greek prepositions: *para, en* and *epi*. Which mean: 'alongside', 'in', and 'upon'.

Para. The Holy Spirit is a courting Spirit. He comes alongside and draws us to Christ. He comes *para* to us.

En. The moment we receive Jesus into our lives, the Holy Spirit fills us, and dwells in us. He dwells *en* us. He begins that work of transformation. He is the indwelling Spirit.

Epi. Still, there is more. Jesus says you will receive power when the Holy Spirit comes upon you, when he overflows you. This is the sense of the word *epi*.

Our lives are not just vessels containing the Spirit. They're channels, conduits, through which the Spirit flows to touch the world around us. The experience of the overflow of the Holy Spirit, which we see particularly in the Acts of the Apostles, provides evidence of the *dunamos* – the power of God, active and alive amongst us.

So, what happens, when you wait, is that he will overflow you with the Holy Spirit. And the knowledge you have about Jesus becomes more than knowledge: it means you begin to live Jesus, it means that Jesus pours out of you – his character, his style, his compassion, his mercy, his love, his world obsession. It's the presence of the Holy Spirit that does this.

I'm not sure we really get how crucial he is.

Jesus does. Just before he goes, Jesus introduces the Holy Spirit to his disciples:

> 'But very truly I tell you, it is for your good that I am going away. Unless I go away, the Advocate will not come to you; but if I go, I will send him to you. When he comes, he will prove the world to be in the wrong about sin and righteousness and judgment: about sin, because people do not believe in me; about righteousness, because I am going to the Father, where you can see me no longer; and about judgment, because the prince of this world now stands condemned.
>
> 'I have much more to say to you, more than you can now bear. But when he, the Spirit of truth, comes, he will guide you into all the truth. He will not speak on his own; he will speak only what

he hears, and he will tell you what is yet to come. He will glorify me because it is from me that he will receive what he will make known to you. All that belongs to the Father is mine. That is why I said the Spirit will receive from me what he will make known to you.'

John 16:7–15

Very carefully and clearly, Jesus tells us that it is better for us that we have the Holy Spirit with us. Better even than if *Jesus himself* were physically here with us. This is an incredible statement. Who can this Holy Spirit be? What must he be like?

Jesus calls the Holy Spirit 'the Advocate'. This is the Scottish word for barrister – someone who argues your case or represents you. He speaks to us on behalf of Jesus and the Father, and he speaks on our behalf to the Lord.

And Jesus tells us that he is the Spirit of truth. He assures us that he will guide us into all truth. The Holy Spirit helps us see and recognise what is true, he helps us know what is true, he helps us understand what is true, and he helps us speak what is true. He helps us *be* true. He convicts of lies and falsehood. His is a searing truth, a sword-like truth. Truth in a world of lies, of 'economies with the truth'. Truth in a world of relative truth. Clarity and objective reality. Jesus says he is the Spirit of truth.

And what is true is Jesus, all that he said, all that he did, all that he taught. That is why only the Holy Spirit can draw people to Jesus, can make the blind see.

The Holy Spirit is the Spirit of Jesus.

3 FOR 1 GOD

Ruach

In the Old Testament the Holy Spirit is called *Ruach*. *Ruach* is a kind of raw, wild wind. He blows where he will. He goes where he chooses.

In the New Testament, in Jesus, *Ruach* has a face. He has a personality. He is called the Spirit of Jesus, for example in Acts 16:7 and Philippians 1:19. It is the Spirit of Jesus that draws us and keeps us in intimate relationship with the God who is Father, Son and Holy Spirit. He is the one who reveals truth and keeps us in truth. He empowers us. He breathes life into *Abba's* children.

So here's what I need you to understand. Just as Father is God; just as Jesus is God; be under no illusion: it is clear in the Scriptures, the Holy Spirit is absolutely, completely, utterly God. And although they are three distinct persons, God the Father, God the Son and God the Holy Spirit, we need to understand they are a unity. You can't separate Father, Son and Holy Spirit. You can't choose to worship the Father and the Son and not worship the Holy Spirit.

We see that throughout the whole of Scripture.

At creation

In the beginning, at creation, God the Father was there, creating. In the beginning, at creation, Jesus was there. And in the beginning, at creation, the Holy Spirit was there, hovering, *brooding* across the face of the waters. The Hebrew word is '*rachaph*', it means he reproduces, he creates, and he births something. The Holy Spirit is the divine midwife. I love this picture of coming pregnancy, a picture of creativity, a picture of the creative expression of the Godhead. So Father, Son and Holy Spirit, in creation.

- Father: 'In the beginning God created the heavens and the earth' (Genesis 1:1)
- Son: 'Through him all things were made; without him nothing was made that has been made' (John 1:3)
- Spirit: 'the Spirit of God was hovering over the waters' (Genesis 1:2)

In the incarnation

And in the incarnation, when Jesus comes into the world, you see Father, Son and Holy Spirit in perfect unity. The Father sends Jesus to be the atoning sacrifice, and Jesus says, 'the Son can do nothing by himself; he can do only what he sees his Father doing' (John 5:19). He is born with the power of the Holy Spirit and when he is baptised the Holy Spirit alights on him as a dove. It is in the Holy Spirit that he is sent into the desert, and his ministry is in the power of the Holy Spirit. Father, Son and Holy Spirit.

- Father: 'For God so loved the world that he gave his one and only Son' (John 3:16)
- Son: 'The Word became flesh and made his dwelling among us' (John 1:14)
- Spirit: 'This is how the birth of Jesus the Messiah came about: his mother Mary was pledged to be married to Joseph, but before they came together, she was found to be pregnant through the Holy Spirit' (Matthew 1:18)

At the birth of the church

At the commissioning of the church, when Jesus tells the disciples to go into all the world, preach and teach and make disciples, he also says *'As the Father has sent me, I am sending you'*. Then he breathes on them and they receive the Holy Spirit. In Acts 2 tongues of fire come down upon the church. The Holy Spirit is given so that Jesus people might look like Jesus and continue the work of Jesus being the bride of Jesus and bringing the kingdom of God. Father, Son and Holy Spirit.

- Father: 'As the Father has sent me …' (John 20:21a)
- Son: '… I am sending you' (John 20:21b)
- Spirit: And with that he breathed on them and said, 'Receive the Holy Spirit' (John 20:22)

So we can't get away with thinking that we are 'Father-centred', or 'Jesus-centred', or 'Holy Spirit-centred'. You can't separate one from the others. It is as if they are in an eternal dance, one with another – this is how some Eastern Orthodox theologians, such as Gregory of Nazianzus, described it.

Yet there's something about the Holy Spirit.

There's something deeply attractive and mystical, something magnificent about the Holy Spirit. And there is something incredibly controversial and weird about the Holy Spirit. This person of God has often been seen as a marginal, lesser figure of the Trinity. He's been spurned, even rejected. Some of us just don't want to talk about him or worship him. We understand the Father, we know the Son, but the Holy Spirit – that's for extremists, fanatics. For many of us, the fullness of the Holy Spirit is something we aspire to only in theory. In practice, we are deeply troubled. We have more questions than answers and we find ourselves closed off to God's incredible power.

The Puritan Writer, John Owen, in his work on the Holy Spirit said:

From the beginning of the world, the principle revelation that God made of himself, was the unity of his nature, and his sovereignty overall; and herein the person of the Father was immediately represented, with his power and authority. In this state of things, the only apostasy of the church could be polytheism and idolatry. ...

Again they were tried with a new dispensation. The Son of God was sent to them in the flesh. To receive and obey him was now to be the principal instance and trial of their faith. Here, also, the greater part of that church and people fell by their unbelief; apostatised from God (and became thereby neither church nor people ... the Son of God calls and gathers another church; founding it on his own person, with faith, and the profession of it therein (Matt 16:18-19) In this new church, this foundation is fixed: 'That Jesus Christ, the Son of God, is to be honoured even as we honour the Father.' ...

But now Christ being ascended to his Father, has committed all his affairs in the Church and the world to the Holy Spirit (John 16:7), and with this design, that the person of the Spirit may be singularly exalted in the Church. Wherefore, the duty of the church now, immediately respects the Spirit of God, who acts towards it in the name of the Father and of the Son ... for the sin of despising his person and rejecting his work now is of the same nature with the idolatry of old, and the Jews' rejection of the person of the son.

John Owen, *The Holy Spirit: His gifts and power*,
Christian Focus, Scotland, 2004

TRANSFORMED

Look at the change in this group of believers. At first, 'fearful' doesn't begin to describe it; 'petrified' is more like it. They didn't know what to do when Jesus was arrested. We criticise Peter for his denial, but at least Peter stayed, he followed. The others ran away.

Peter, James and John, Thomas, Simon the Zealot and their mates – these guys give me encouragement really, because they are numpties. Get this: they ask, 'Lord, are you at this time going to restore the kingdom to Israel?' (Acts 1:6). These men have walked with Jesus, listened to Jesus' teaching, seen Jesus' miracles. They've been closer to Jesus than anybody else – and they *still* don't get it. And they ask, in effect, 'Are you going to come in power, are you going to kick out the Romans, are you going to restore our nation?' No, no, no. They just didn't understand Jesus.

But then the Holy Spirit comes. And does something incredible.

Look at Peter. Peter has standout potential, but he's in danger of allowing fear to take him out. Then he meets the forgiveness of Jesus and the power of the Holy Spirit. His life gets transformed when the Holy Spirit comes. Remember, a few days before, warming himself by a fire, he'd sworn, 'I don't know this man you're talking about' (Mark 14:71). This same Peter stands up and speaks. And publicly, in front of thousands, Peter gives what is probably the clearest sermon on the person and identity of Jesus Christ that we have in the New Testament. Something must have happened.

Clearly much has. He's met with the resurrected Jesus and he's been re-commissioned. But it would appear to be this encounter with the Holy Spirit that is the game-changer.

The Holy Spirit brings clarity about Jesus, the truth of who he is. It's the Holy Spirit who will reveal Jesus to you so that suddenly it begins to make sense; it's not that everything falls into place. But it is that you get it. It's the transforming power of the Holy Spirit that will enable you to be very bold about Jesus. And the power of the Holy Spirit is going to cause you to co-operate with the Godhead's world obsession: Jerusalem, Judea, Samaria and the ends of the earth.

The Holy Spirit has not been sent to us just so that we can enjoy life – the anointing that we have is not just so that we can have a fantastic worship service and some interesting and powerful teaching. The Spirit's anointing for you is the same anointing that Jesus had, it is the anointing to be good news to the poor and recovery of sight to the blind, to heal the sick and to raise the dead and to cleanse the lepers, and to show people that the kingdom of God is now, so we can say, 'It's amongst you, it's here. Let me show you'.

The anointing is for transformation, of me, you and everyone else. And it is supposed to be tangible, you are supposed to be able to see it.

DO BE DO BE DO BE DO ...

The foundation and essence of that transformation consists in what we do and who we are. The Lord wants us to bear fruit. He wants us to look more like Jesus.

The apostle Paul speaks about the fruit of the Holy Spirit – it is a beautiful description of the Jesus life.

This is going to make all the difference in the world, for the world. What would it look like if those around us saw more love? More joy, peace, patience? Kindness? Self-control? Imagine what that would be like. What if we truly let the Holy Spirit have us and fill us? Imagine the fruit! Imagine the impact!

You see this is the only way we can see fruit. However hard we try, we can't produce fruit. We just can't whip it up and push it out. Fruit bearing is organic, not binary. A pear tree does not produce a pear by busting its own butt to push a pear out. A pear is the natural result of the right environment and the right care. It's what a pear tree is for. It's what a pear tree does.

Sons see fruit. They just do. It's what they do. They see fruit because they are fathered, because they are one with Christ and because they are full of the Holy Spirit. This is divine co-operation. This is you and I welcomed into a relationship with the Holy Spirit of God. And this incredible union results in wonderful and beautiful fruit. Fruit that changes you and everyone around you.

He gives gifts to his people. He gifts his leaders to be apostles, prophets, evangelists, pastors and teachers, so that all God's people might be equipped to serve, that we might be the Body of Christ. His gifts are for all, they are supernatural and they are varied. The lists in the Bible – you'll find them in Romans 12, 1 Corinthians 12 and Ephesians 4 – are just examples.

He gives his fruit so that we might be like Jesus and his gifts so that we might act like Jesus. You see, in the economy of the Spirit, fruit and gifts, being and doing are not 'either or' options, but 'both and' opportunities.

The problem of course is that many in the Church, so many of us, have settled for less than any of this and we miss out on fruit and gifts. You and I need more of him. We need this fullness, this fruitfulness, so we can look like Jesus.

The Holy Spirit has so much to give us. He gives creativity, visions, dreams. He moves in the miraculous. He gives new ministries of compassion. He inspires fresh expressions of church. He's utterly contemporary, ultimately relevant, and yet steeped in tradition.

MISSING OUT

So why do we miss out? Because we do so often, don't we. It's not rational.

Some of us think the work of the Holy Spirit was for a previous time, a past time. Perhaps we are more comfortable with scientific and rational explanations for the supernatural. We may have accepted the argument that we were filled with the Holy Spirit as we recognised and acknowledged Jesus as Saviour, and that this was the only purpose for the Spirit.

But this just doesn't make sense. Why would he fill us if he didn't intend to work with and through us?

Some of us miss out purely because of fear. It's messy, and you can't control it. Maybe you had a bad experience, someone exaggerated, someone pushed you over when they prayed for you, or you saw someone acting strangely. And it all felt a little bit put on. Abusive. Perhaps it is more than that. Perhaps you trusted your career or your future on a word or a dream and it didn't work out well. Perhaps people prayed for healing for someone you loved and they died. Perhaps you've heard a lot of talk about miracles, but you've never actually seen one.

And now it is just too difficult to have anything to do with God the Holy Spirit. It is easier to be careful, or even cynical. You fear being out of control so you try to avoid that particular scenario and consequently don't give him space. Instead you prefer to focus on what you can understand.

But the Holy Spirit is not to be feared. In fact, it grieves his heart. The Holy Spirit brings order – as we see in Genesis 1 – but it is always his order, and rarely our order. Sometimes it might look a bit messy, but he is God. He is not to be feared, not to be ignored and not to be avoided. He is not to be controlled either. He is to be embraced and surrendered to and given room to.

So, back to Acts 2. The disciples are all together, waiting, praying. And then the Holy Spirit shows up and they go crazy. They get bold. There is this uninhibited witness. They get drunk on the Holy Spirit. Which is what people thought had happened, they thought they were mad, crazy mad, that they must be drunk. So Peter has to explain, 'These people are not drunk, as you suppose. It's only nine in the morning!' (Acts 2:15).

Drunk people do crazy things. They don't care what other people think. They lose their fear of man, they are not concerned about humiliation, and they are not worried about the consequences. In Ephesians 5:18, Paul repeats the comparison: 'Do not get drunk on wine, … Instead, be filled with the Spirit', or, literally, 'be being filled'. Don't be drunk with wine, but be drunk with the Holy Spirit. Because God wants to remove the clothing of control that you have, that debilitates you. That keeps you from standing. That keeps you from the freedom of his control. He wants to cloak you with power, and you're going to do crazy.

Sometimes I think God has to offend our religious sensitivities to free us and use us. Sometimes we are so controlled, we are only allowing God to do what we have already reasoned that he can already do. Who is God in that? We don't like God to have control of our emotions because we don't like to be out of control – it might get messy and people might think badly of us. But actually the Holy Spirit is God. He's got good things. God wants to remove the clothing of control so that you might preach the kingdom, love outrageously, heal the sick, cleanse the lepers, raise the dead – but only when you get drunk in the Spirit, when you let him be God. When we build community in the power of the Spirit, people will take a look at our community and they will say, 'It's not pretend, it's not superficial, they don't preach what they don't live, they actually love one another. They minister with power, they speak the truth into one another's lives'.

THE MYSTERY OF THE MANIFESTATION

There's a way to deal with this. And you must deal with this if you're going to stand.

Our God meets us and enjoys us individually. We have unique relationships with the Godhead. I have a friend who looks like a windmill and acts like a windmill when the Spirit comes upon her. You may well have a friend like that too. It's loud, it's ungainly, and sometimes it's distracting. But it's real. That's just how she and God delight in each other. So, with all due respect ... *get over it!*

God is going to meet you in the way that is most appropriate to you. Trust him. Do you trust him? Then let him meet you as you are. No one knows you better. Don't settle for part – ask for all. Ask to be filled. It will feel like something. It might look like something.

As we've already said, he is a person. He is personal, ironically the most intimate member of the Trinity. He is 'God at hand'. He is God who is present, God with us.

Which makes sense of the fact that the fullness of the Holy Spirit is also an experience. When writing the Acts of the Apostles, Dr Luke is very clear to document the experience of the presence of the Holy Spirit.

- At Pentecost there was power to witness, as Jesus had promised, and speaking in tongues (Acts 2:4, 11)
- In Samaria there is something so obvious that when Simon the Scorcerer saw it he wanted to buy the power to imitate it (Acts 8:18–19)

- At Paul's conversion, there is boldness and witness (Acts 9:17, 22)
- At the house of Cornelius there was speaking in tongues and praising God (Acts 10:46)
- In Ephesus, where Paul found the disciples of John the Baptist, there was speaking in tongues and prophesying (Acts 19:6)

Throughout Acts the filling of the Holy Spirit is usually followed and evidenced by the working of miracles, signs and wonders. This adds up to fairly compelling evidence that when you are full of the Holy Spirit you will know it, and so will others around you.

The Holy Spirit is a person. But being filled with him is an experience. Encountering him is always an experience.

> *Being filled with the Spirit means to be filled with the immediate presence of God to the extent that you are feeling what God himself feels, desiring what God desires, doing what God wants, speaking by God's power, praying and ministering in God's strength and knowing with the knowledge that God himself gives.*
>
> Wayne Grudem, Being Filled with the Holy Spirit, sermon delivered at Bethlehem Baptist, 23/03/2006 as quoted on http://www.fundamentallyreformed.com

The Holy Spirit is not to be passed down like some ancient tradition, he needs to be known first hand, a present reality. Throughout Scripture, certain images are used to describe the experience of the Holy Spirit.

He is fire

John the Baptist announced that Jesus would baptise with the Holy Spirit and with fire. Fire is powerful, overwhelming. Luke records this on the day of Pentecost as the Holy Spirit was given: something like tongues of fire came to rest on the believers. Fire purifies, cauterises: let the Holy Spirit be Lord and he will begin to burn off anything that is not Jesus, anything that is not really you.

He is water

Water is often used as a metaphor of the activity of the Spirit. It speaks of life, as in the picture in Ezekiel 47. The Holy Spirit is the life-bringer. He is the marvellous, creative expression of the Godhead.
The Psalmist writes:

> *He makes springs pour water into the ravines; …*
>
> *He waters the mountains from his upper chambers;*
> *the land is satisfied by the fruit of his work.*
> *He makes grass grow for the cattle,*
> *and plants for people to cultivate –*
> *bringing forth food from the earth:*
> *wine that gladdens human hearts,*
> *oil to make their faces shine,*
> *and bread that sustains their hearts.*
>
> *All creatures look to you*
> *to give them their food at the proper time.*
> *When you give it to them, they gather it up;*
> *when you open your hand, they are satisfied with good things.*
> *When you hide your face, they are terrified;*
> *when you take away their breath, they die and return to the dust.*
> *When you send your Spirit, they are created, and you renew the*
> *face of the ground.*
>
> Psalm 104:10, 13–15, 27–30

Let the Holy Spirit be God and he will begin to renew life in you. Where there is desert, springs of water will flow. Where there is arid faith, there will be abundant fruit.

He is wind

The Holy Spirit is God at hand, but he is not God on tap. You can't turn him off, or turn him on and set him running. He is God. Jesus likens him to the wind: 'The wind blows wherever it pleases' (John 3:8). The Holy Spirit divinely guides, he divinely moves. He wants to lead us into the truth for our lives and the path for our steps. The Holy Spirit is the source of all truth. He gives words to prophets. He inspires Scripture writers. He has existed since the dawn of time, and will exist for eternity and he speaks to us today. He, who is the source of the life of God, is also the source of the knowledge of God.

- God spoke through the prophets of the Old Testament, by the Spirit: 'For prophecy never had its origin in the human will, but prophets, though human, spoke from God as they were carried along by the Holy Spirit' (2 Peter 1:21).
- God speaks through the authors of Scripture, by the Spirit: 'All Scripture is God-breathed' (2 Timothy 3:16).
- God speaks through the preachers of his Word, by the Spirit: 'If anyone speaks they should do so as one who speaks the very words of God' (1 Peter 4:11).

Any division between the Word and the Spirit is nuts! You don't have the Word of God, unless you have the fullness of the Spirit. You don't get the fullness of the Spirit without a passion for, and a commitment to, the Word of God. Let the Holy Spirit be God and he will direct your path. He is speaking always. You will learn to listen and obey.

He is dove

When Jesus is baptised by John in the Jordan, the Holy Spirit descends, in the form of a dove. There is something gentle, peaceful and holy about that image. He is the Dove; he is the tarrying presence of God with us. He is fire and water and wind but he is also the Dove. The Holy Spirit wants to meet with us, live in us and bestow you and I with the continual presence of a holy God who loves us. We need to take care that our charismatic worship events are not just soft rock concerts where the experience of the Holy Spirit is whipped up or emotionally manipulated. No, his presence is so precious that he warrants reverence and space, time and nurture. And not only in time spent in gatherings, but all time. You carry the presence of God as you walk in the fullness of the Spirit of God, always.

Let the Holy Spirit be God and you will know the Father, you will know the Son and you will know you, as you are known by him.

It's what we need, the overflow, and the power. The fire, the water, the wind, the dove, the fruit. You need it so that you might be you. For you and for the world around you. Isn't that what you want? Then have it!

Jesus said, 'If you then, though you are evil, know how to give good gifts to your children, how much more will your Father in heaven give the Holy Spirit to those who ask him!' (Luke 11:13).

—————————— SO: ——————————

- Read Acts 2. Try to see that this is 'normal'. It is a wonderful account of a special moment in the life of the Church, but it is also God's 'normal'. It's what your normal could be. Spend some time thanking the Father for the Holy Spirit.

- Get honest with the Holy Spirit.
  I am afraid because . . .
  I have reservations about . . .
  Is there any part of what you believe about the Holy Spirit that might make you less than open to receiving more of God? If you suspect those beliefs to be wrong, ask forgiveness for them.

- If you can, find someone in whom you can see evidence of fullness in the Holy Spirit. Ask them to pray for you, to pray for more of God. Ask the Holy Spirit to reveal areas in your life that he wants to sanctify and to help you bear fruit. Ask for gifts. Our God loves to give good gifts!

- God speaks; he is speaking, all the time. Are you listening? Sometimes he shouts, at other times he whispers. Often he nudges, regularly he prompts. How are you responding? You see, your Holy Spirit responder muscles need developing just like your pecs and your guns, or you get spiritual moobs or bingo wings. Resolve to speculate on his voice, his nudge. If he asks you to speak, to bless, to share, to write, to confront, to encourage, to go, to stay. Do it, do it today! And tell someone else, so you might be encouraged and accountable.

Read on ...

5.

NOT YET NOW

SOMETHING ABOUT PURPOSE

The Ultimate Answer to Life, The Universe, and Everything is ... 42!
The Hitchhiker's Guide to the Galaxy, Douglas Adams
(1978)

•

To be what we are, and to become what we are capable of becoming, is the only end of life.
Familiar Studies of Men and Books, Robert Louis Stevenson
(1882)

•

To the person who pleases him, God gives wisdom, knowledge and happiness, but to the sinner he gives the task of gathering and storing up wealth to hand it over to the one who pleases God. This too is meaningless, a chasing after the wind.
Ecclesiastes 2:26

What are you for? Why are we here? What is the meaning of it all? What is the meaning of me? Huge, huge questions, being asked internally all the time by people who know there must be more. A greater explanation. A bigger story. Is there more to life than education, exams, taxes, kids, jobs, money, housework, relationships, retirement and death? Crass questions, but asked nonetheless by all of us.

Here's the thing. You will never find true purpose in life outside of God, Father God. You will never find your purpose outside of his Son, he is the essence of your humanity. You will never find your purpose outside of the Holy Spirit. He is the bringer of your life.

God is the Creator. You are his creation. You and I were created to walk with God. More than that, we were designed to walk in rhythm with him. We were designed to walk in his direction, to know him intimately and to enjoy him fully. We were created to be in unity with him. We were created to co-operate with his purposes. We were created for a purpose.

RUNNING

And yet ironically you and I are somehow predisposed to run away from God. And we do. We find ourselves running from him. We've all done it. At some point in our lives, and even day to day, we choose to run, to hide from God, or to avoid him. Sometimes it's deliberate and open. Sometimes our actions have been much subtler than that – a sort of subconscious avoiding. We don't admit it to ourselves but before we know it, we just end up doing our own thing.

Maybe it was the way we were raised. Maybe we didn't like our school, our work, or our church. Maybe something went badly wrong in our lives. Maybe we were treated badly by someone who was supposed to represent God. We thought: 'If that is what God is like …' (You fill in the dots – you know what you thought.) At some stage in life, most of us ran away from God. And when we did, Father God, in his grace, let us go.

When we run away from God he doesn't stop us. He doesn't coerce obedience and loyalty from us. Free will is his genuine gift to us. He wants us to freely love and serve him. He isn't in the business of forcing love on us. Because forced love is not love, it is something altogether different. God lets us go. But there are consequences. When we run from God, our lives begin to unravel. Maybe the unravelling doesn't come immediately. Maybe things seem fine for a while. But when we are out of synch with Father God, a clock is ticking. Sooner or later independence will bite us. Things will go sour. Sooner, or later, others will be affected by the shrapnel of our exploding lives.

Why am I so sure of this? Because when we run from God, we run from the source of all wisdom, love and purpose. We run from the God who loves us, knows us and who has a bespoke plan for each of our lives. We cut loose. And when we do, where does our wisdom come from? From culture? From feelings and hunches? How do you work out and live out purpose in your life? Possibly the saddest thing of all is to live your whole life doing the best you can, yet never knowing, or truly experiencing, your purpose.

What is that purpose? It's been debated across the ages and libraries are filled with musings on this subject, but our purpose is much simpler than it seems.

Our purpose is to know God.

Our purpose is to know God, the *true* God, the God that we've just described, the Father, the Son and the Holy Spirit. But it's also to relate to him in such a way that he receives glory and to participate in his plan of redemption. It is to love the people that he loves. Your neighbour. Your brother. It's to love the world that he made.

THE GARDEN

Let's go back to the beginning. Back to the garden.

The garden was beautiful. The garden was perfection. God had created it, and it was flawless. But the garden gets busted wide open.

Satan slides up in the form of a serpent and attempts to convince Eve that evil is really good and that what God says is actually bad. Eve listens to the dark whisper. She believes the lie. She is convinced she will never truly live until she renounces the authority of her Father God. Soon Adam buys the lie. They eat the fruit. The garden is broken. The world is a mess. Sin has taken hold. The mood becomes dark. The world falls into a state of theological bankruptcy. Human beings turn away from God in rebellion and he turns away in holiness. We can no longer walk in the same way in the garden. We hide. He judges.

Separation.

Creation and creator are out of relationship. Perfect trust and intimacy are gone. Things unravel quickly. Adam and Eve start to judge one another. It's the same sin of judgment that you and I engage in continually. They blame each other and that pattern is set. Generation after generation seeks to find someone else to take the heat. Blame is embedded in the genes. The Human Race struggles with relationships.

Shame pours in. Adam and Eve make coverings to hide their nakedness. This damaged world leaves them no longer comfortable in their own skins. We no longer know who we are. We identify ourselves by what is said about us, spoken over us. We form an identity through what we wear. What dress size we are starts to matter. The stuff we own. Are we hot, or are we not? Popularity matters, really matters. And we are just not comfortable in our own skin. The environment unravels. The harmony between the created order and humanity is over. The relationship between man and the world created for him is spoiled.

And the root of all this? Sin.

We are busted.

The fact that humans took this free will and used it to decide not to follow the Creator doesn't take God by surprise – after all he's the omniscient God. And because he's God, he's creating a response to this tragedy. Even this most devastating of moments simply forms the backdrop and context for the most wonderful and beautiful rescue plan ever conceived. Even here, there is a prophecy; there is a picture of how this rescue will take place. There is to be a crushing and a covering and a restoration of all things (check out Genesis 3:15).

And in all this, our true purpose in life is set. It's to know restoration and to participate in the restoration of all things. It's to know God and make him known. It's to know intimacy with a God who wants intimacy. It's to know ourselves, to love ourselves and consequently to have the ability to really worship God and really love others too.

Our purpose is to love this planet, to love this people and to work for the restoration of all things.

THE WHOLE BANG SHOOT

Colossians 1:19. 'For God was pleased to have all his fullness dwell in him, and through him to reconcile to himself all things . . .' That word 'all' in the original Greek means, not surprisingly, all. It means everything, the whole bang shoot.

For the most part, the way the evangelical church has understood the Gospel has been limited. We understand that 'I am sinful, but God loves me so much that he sent Jesus to die for me, so that I might not perish but have life.' That's not wrong. It's great. But when a church gets missional, it begins to view this slightly differently. We begin to see, 'God loves me so much (and those around me) that he sent Jesus to die for me (for us), so that we can be forgiven and live with him forever.'

But even that is just a reduction of the Gospel. We have taken something really big and made it more ... *manageable.* It's more than me, my mates and Jesus. It's more than sin, salvation, and heaven. See, the gospel is not two parts. It is not:

1. We sinned.
2. We get saved.

Really, it's more like four parts.

1. God loves and creates.
2. We rebel and revolt.
3. Jesus comes to save and make a way for forgiveness and eternal life.
4. God is restoring all things. And the story continues ...

So as we are being loved, we are being invited to become conduits in this love – giving it to the world. God is putting this world right through Jesus and an integral part of that plan is to use Jesus' body – the Church. You and I find ourselves in the centre of the divine repair plan for this cosmos. This is purpose.

So, God is not calling us out of the world. He's calling us into it. He is calling us to unleash the compassion of God. He's asking us to heal the sick and love the lost. He's calling us to work for systemic good. To feed the hungry and redeem commerce. To encourage the arts. To bless the good and stand against the unjust. He calls us to live, embrace and declare the kingdom of God and introduce people to a redefined love – a love embodied in Jesus. He wants us to expect and to welcome the power, compassion and creativity of the Holy Spirit. We are called and enabled to be at the heart of God's transformation plans, as his hands, feet and spokespersons. We are called to work in creating and redeeming, transforming and cultivating culture. We are called to be active in the kingdom. We are encouraged to be fully hands on.

Now that sounds like purpose.

IT'S HERE

Jesus comes into this broken world, bringing healing and wholeness, forgiveness and transformation. He brings freedom. He does this in a world where he has to compete with evil and institutionalised religion. Greedy, unjust, business corporations. Caste systems that speak value over people designed to be equal by God. Jesus speaks into this context and calls us to work with him.

The kingdom is here. One day, the kingdom will be all there is. There will be no distraction, no opposition, no warping of God's design. But for now, he calls us to live with him in this shadowland. Work with him in this tension. Embrace the kingdom now. Embrace its values now. Embrace its beauty now. And as we do this, we look for and hope for and pray for the kingdom to come. Wait, with baited breath – for this is our purpose.

The kingdom is living in the not yet now, knowing that the not yet is still to come.

What a calling! The problem is we seem so unwilling to do this. We wait and often we do nothing. We hold on firmly to the gospel *about* Jesus and forget about the gospel *of* Jesus.

The Grand Old Duke

Do you remember the nursery song 'The Grand Old Duke of York?' He had ten thousand men. He was in the business of marching them up and down hills. He had issues with positioning and liked to clarify if they were 'up', 'down', or perhaps, 'neither up, nor down'. You know the man.

Most nursery songs have a deeper meaning. I guess traditionally the Grand Old Duke rhyme is supposed to remind us of the need for a clear purpose, for single-mindedness. But our journey in God is, paradoxically, a journey going in *two* directions at the same time. It is a journey up the hill to God and a journey down the valley into the world. It's a life of living the mountaintop experience in the depths of the valley. Which would be impossible if he wasn't God, but he is and it is what he calls us to do. The trouble is that many Jesus followers want to walk one way. Or the other. A few are willing to walk one route *and then* the other. But very, very few want to tackle both directions at the same time. So the church gets stuck halfway up a hill, and becomes no more use than … well … a church stuck halfway up a hill.

The call of the purposeful is *both* to intimacy and to involvement. To relationship and responsibility. To stand in the valley, in light of the mountain. It is to love God and to love people and to realise that these two are never in competition with one another. This dual goal is perfectly harmonious. It is perfect rhythm. It is to pray, 'Your kingdom come. Your will be done on earth as it is in heaven.' It is to live 'Your kingdom come', and bring heaven to earth.

Our purpose is to seek first the kingdom of God. So what is the kingdom of God? What are we seeking? The rule, and reign of Jesus. The place and time where who Jesus is, and what Jesus wants, happen. Because he is the king.

Our purpose is worship and restoration. Worshipful restoration.

The kingdom is

Luke 4. Jesus' first sermon. Remember? The kingdom will not be owned, controlled, managed, reduced by Jesus' relatives and hometown Nazareth. Nor indeed by us. The kingdom is not something to be achieved. Which means, in our achievement-oriented world, that comprehending and living out this kingdom is tricky for us. We want to order and achieve and run our spiritual lives. We want control and planned outcomes. Our bookshops are full of self-help manuals, books that promise '*Seven ways to …*' or '*Four plans to …*', books that promise spiritual achievement, growing your church or taking things to the next level. Whatever that means.

We can't plan or grow it – the kingdom will grow imperceptibly and unstoppably, like mustard seed or yeast in dough (Luke

13:18–21). We can't analyse it or predict it (Luke 17:20–21). We can't own it or tame it, for it belongs to little children and the poor. The kingdom of heaven is to be embraced, so tightly, that heaven oozes out of you. It's to embrace the kingdom so that heaven's peace, heaven's justice, heaven's love and heaven's power is a reality that you and I walk in.

In this kingdom what God wants, happens. Justice and mercy happen. Peace and restoration happen. Perfect identity happens. Restored relationships happen. A new heaven and a new earth happen. His presence happens constantly. What is our part in the kingdom now? It's to bring heaven to earth right now, as the Spirit of Jesus works in us to bring healing and comfort and freedom.

In this kingdom of heaven who God is, is evident. In my decisions and my actions. In my speech I bring something of the reality of the atmosphere of heaven. How I spend my money is directed by heaven's values of love and justice more than earth's values of acquisition and greed. How I speak to and of others is shot through with the language and heart attitude of heaven rather than the harsh, demeaning and critical spirit of earth.

What does it look like? You join the dots. There are countless examples of the potential of heaven invading earth in your life and in mine. The kingdom is, let it come.

The kingdom is now

We walk in this now, not later. We are not to wait anymore, not to hold on for heaven. The kingdom is a declaration and a demonstration that heaven's agenda and heaven's orientation is now – here! Of course it's not yet. But in the kingdom, not yet is also right now!

Personal Purpose

God knows everything about us. He's the God of every detail. He's the God who is there in any and every moment. Father

God is in the depths and in the heights, as we read in Psalm 139. He's a God who thinks of each of us. His thoughts on us outweigh the billions of grains of sand on the seashore. He is the God of that much detail. Paul says that Father God even knows where you and I will live one day (Acts 17:26).

So if God can number the hairs on our heads, if God thinks of us constantly, can you honestly accept that the extent of his plan for you is something like this: 'Go to school – get good grades – go to university – get a good job, so you can earn good money – buy a big house with mono-block drive and two flat screen TVs – have a 4×4 in the drive – make sure you're in the right catchment area for a good school so your kids can follow in these, your limited footsteps – then make sure they follow the same plan.' Is that really it? Or, do you think there might be more?

Live in the not yet *now*. The kingdom is here.

---------------------------------- SO: ----------------------------------

- It starts on our knees; you've got to want no other king, nor any other kingdom. It starts with prayer; we only discover what God is up to when we ask him, when we come alongside. Prayer unlocks our spiritual eyes. So here is the prayer. Will you pray it with me?

Lord, have my heart – change my heart, my attitudes. May my heart start to beat in time with yours, may my attitudes begin to reflect yours.

Lord open my eyes – help me see this world differently, the way you see it. Help me see and love people the way you do. May I see your creation in a new way. Renew my resolve to steward well all that you have given. Help me see the city, the town where you have placed me as you see it.

Lord move my feet – send me to represent you. Release my hands, my tongue, my wallet and my life to embrace your reign and live your kingdom, its beauty and wonder.

Father may your kingdom come – now – through me.

- One of the great joys Niki and I have in our discipling ministry is to run discipleship boot camps for students in our house. As we teach leadership skills, spiritual disciplines and missional discipleship, we give out regular challenges. One of those challenges is to write five rules for your life and then to share them with the group. We have had some amazing evenings hearing, laughing and praying around these rules. If you are going to find and walk in purpose, then you are going to need some disciplines.

  Spend some time thinking about what five rules you would choose. Write them down and share them with one other trusted friend.

You might also like to read:

This Beautiful Mess, Rick McKinley (Multnomah 2006)

6.

THAT'S MY BOY

... eye contact is the most intimacy two people can have – forget sex – because the optic nerve is technically an extension of the brain, and when two people look into each other's eyes, it's brain-to-brain.

Hey Nostradamus!, Douglas Coupland (2004)

•

You know when I sit and when I rise;
*   you perceive my thoughts from afar.*
You discern my going out and my lying down;
*   you are familiar with all my ways.*
Before a word is on my tongue
*   you, LORD, know it completely.*
You hem me in behind and before,
*   and you lay your hand upon me.*

Psalm 139:2–5

When I see Father God face to face, I don't want to hear him say, 'Well done good and faithful servant.' I don't. Seriously. I mean, imagine if your dad said that to you? It would be like you were *really* in trouble! Or it would mean you had a really odd, dysfunctional relationship.

When I see Father God, I want to hear him say 'That's my boy!' And I want him to bear hug me with that 'Daddy hug' and then wrestle me to the ground and pin me down.

LOVE IS...

Jesus put on flesh, set his face towards a cross, went through utter agony at Gethsemane and Golgotha. So that we would obey him? No. He didn't die so that we would respect him, and sing songs to him. No. He did it so that we could be fully restored, back in relationship with the Father, real relationship, walking in the garden in the evening, talking about real stuff. He did it for love.

This story that we now find ourselves in is, quite simply, a love story. It's an epic love story. It's a story of the Father's heart, of his pursuit of our hearts. For God *so loved* the world. It's *the* love story. It's the story of the Prodigal Son, lived out again and again in our lives. It's the story of a God who says, 'Call me Daddy. I'm your Papa. I love you with a perfect love. I love you because I love you, because I love you.' His is grace-love. A love that says 'I want to know you and I want you to know me.' A love that says, 'Come and walk with me, in the garden.' It's intimacy in its purest form. The Holy Spirit is calling us into deeper intimacy. This is not a transaction. This is not a 'If you pray, then I will come' deal (although sometimes he does seem to say that). It's a relationship in which he comes to us. He embraces us. And by his Spirit, he dwells with us.

At a recent gathering of leaders there was great expectancy. There was a feeling that God was going to do something significant; he was going to speak to his people. Sure enough, someone approached the platform with a prophetic word for those gathered. The senior leader was excited. The man gave the prophetic word: 'Father God says, "I've really missed you. I'm looking forward to spending time with you."' The leader confessed that he was really disappointed with what he heard.

Do we love God? Do we even like him? Be honest.

We say we love Jesus. At least on Sundays. We say it in song-singing time; we say it in the prayers. If we aren't thinking of lunch or something. Yet most days almost everything else in life seems to take priority. The Gym. Football. TV. Sleeping in. Church business meetings. Choices and priorities. This tells us something. The choices and the actions of our daily lives reveal our true passions.

Sociologists have recognised and named a recent cultural phenomenon. FOMO. Fear of missing out. The syndrome creates addicts, people addicted to facebook, twitter, snapchat, or whatever the latest social media craze happens to be. It keeps us glued to screens, 'constantly' in touch. I'm sure it has many societal benefits. But we are in real collective danger of ironically 'missing out' on what we are created for, and consequently misunderstanding who we really are. I think I have FOMO. I really fear missing out on intimacy with my heavenly Father. The wonderful thing is that still, through the distractions and competing priorities, Jesus graciously calls to us, drawing us into intimacy.

In the letters to the churches at the start of Revelation, Jesus is appraising seven churches. These people are Christians. They were Christ-followers. He's writing to his friends. Let's look at the two most commonly taught passages.

There must be more than this

Jesus writes to the church at Ephesus that they are busy and good and sound. He affirms them in this. Then he makes an important statement:

> *'you have forsaken the love you had at first'*
>
> Revelation 2:4

He is saying to his people, it's intimacy I'm after, it's love I'm after, it's you I'm after. So return to me as your first choice. Return to me as your first priority. The Bible is clear, from cover to cover. What God desires is not a relationship that is cordial and respectful. Not something distant, based on an event, an appointment, a scheduled meeting ('I come to church, don't I?'). Not a duty, a legal requirement, a financial transaction ('I pay my tithe, don't I?'). It's not how easy I find it to do church! What God is longing for is a relationship that is *intimate*.

We might read the Bible aiming to get things right, to be sound, but to us it's not living or active or doing anything in our lives. We might do our best to learn all about the Holy Spirit, but still, we don't allow his life to overflow, to bubble up and over. We might do homegroup, without doing real life together. We might agree to be leaders or elders, but too often we find the experience dry, crusty. We go through the motions and share our true feelings with no one – because they are all expecting deep spiritual insight from us. We are left thinking 'There must be more than this'.

We might treat Jesus respectfully, but on those terms you and I will never enter into all that God has for us. We will be unfulfilled. We'll never build the kingdom until we open ourselves to intimacy with him – because that's what we were made for.

Here I am

Then, Jesus speaks to his friends in Laodicea. These Christians were very religious. They believed fully in Christ, but they too were reluctant to pursue the level of intimacy that Jesus wants and desires. He says:

> *'I know your deeds, that you are neither cold nor hot. I wish you were either one or the other! So, because you are lukewarm – neither hot nor cold – I am about to spit you out of my mouth.'*
>
> Revelation 3:15, 16

The readers of this letter knew what was being said. Underground pipes brought water from the hot springs of Hieropolis through Laodicea on the way to Colossæ. The water was hot at Hieropolis and therefore useful, cold at Collossæ and therefore refreshing, but tepid at Laodicea, and therefore unpalatable and polluted. The message is unambiguous. They are a good church and good people, but what they offer is not what Jesus wants, or longs for.

You say, 'I am rich; I have acquired wealth and do not need a thing'. But you do not realise that you are wretched, pitiful, poor, blind and naked.

Revelation 3:17

The Laodiceans think they are rich because things are going well. They're seeing growth. They have certain things. They think these things are good. But Jesus tells them they are 'wretched, pitiful, poor, blind'. He spells it out:

'Here I am! I stand at the door and knock. If anyone hears my voice and opens the door, I will come in and eat with that person, and they with me.'

Revelation 3:20

He is saying, *I want you to know me. Here I am. Right here. Let me in.* But these are Christian people. What in the world is Jesus doing outside? Why is he knocking?

This helps us to understand something crucial, something fundamental. God, the Almighty, Creator, has all the power in the universe. Yet there is one thing he has decided that he cannot do. It's the one thing he desires most. He will not make us love him. He cannot, will not, make us love him. Ever. Forced love is no love at all. What he wants is intimacy.

BACK TO THE GARDEN

In the Garden of Eden we had it, before the fall. At the folding up of history we will have it again. But he wants and desires it now. He deeply wants intimacy with you, and with me. It's what we are created for.

Too often we have opted for religion instead of intimacy. We choose it because it allows us to keep God at a distance and treat him respectfully. But this is a very empty thing. Embrace religion and God becomes a formula. We go to church and we sing songs and we do wrong things and then we ask forgiveness. God erases our sin and we share our faith because someone once told us it was right to do that. We are very respectful but there is no intimacy. It's a religion and you know what happens to religious people? Eventually our beliefs become incredibly self-centred and God has to do things for me and it's all about me and my health, and my wealth, and my kids, and my church. And it's a formula and then eventually it becomes judgmental, because we see people doing things that we have decided they should not do, (usually based upon our religious relationship with God). And we respond to these people in a very ungodly way, we end up not liking them. We don't like them because they are 'ungodly'. Ironic that! Even more ironic is that sometimes, secretly, deep down, we just wish we could be as ungodly as them. Because we already feel ungodly and they seem to be having a lot more fun!

Father God has a different way for us – thankfully! Father God is wooing us into intimacy.

And that's what I want. Honestly, that's what I want to want to want. And yet I find it so hard, just God and me. I have tried to journal so often, so many new year's resolutions; so many fresh new leather bound journals for fresh new intimacy attempts. I realised quite recently that I was writing diary entries for the person who would find it when I was dead (happy thought I know). Ridiculous! God wants you, just you, just you and him. And real you and him. He can handle it. Start by telling him why you love him. I find it helps.

Here's the fascinating thing. Father God calls you to intimacy because he just loves you and loves hanging out with you. It's not for anything more complex – it's just for the sake of you and him. So much of what we call worship is not actually about you and him. It gets tainted by my performance and insecurity and approval. One of the most wonderful moments I have ever experienced in public worship was at the climax of a conference in a well-known London church. The vicar stood and led the congregation in singing in the spirit. Not my usual experience and initially a bit strange. But there was something so beautiful and powerful about being together, not understanding the detail of the intimate expression of hundreds of you and him times. Just enjoying him and loving everyone else enjoying him.

It's just about you and him. Yet it will propel you into mission. See when it is about you and him, it very quickly becomes about you and him and everyone else. It will propel you into mission. It just has to! But if you are not intimate with God then you will have very little to give. You have very little to share.

UNLESS YOU EAT, NOBODY GETS TO EAT

One day I found myself lying on the floor of a church. I don't often get visions, but this one was crystal clear. Jesus was walking me up the road – and it was as if I was blindfolded. He was walking backwards, holding both of my hands and yet I could see everything. It was a road I knew well, the road into town. And I kept seeing people I knew. The man in the supermarket. The lady who begs on the street. Jesus was being very friendly, (as you would guess), but he wasn't actually changing their lives. They were left as they were. And I was getting more and more peeved with Jesus. He turned to me and said, 'Shall we go somewhere to eat?' Without hesitating, I said 'Yes'. (Those of you who know me will have no surprise.) He took me to Costa Coffee and I asked 'Who's paying?' (Once again, no surprise.) Jesus said nothing but just produced food from somewhere – haggis, pralines-and-cream ice cream and red wine, three of my favourite foods – how did he know? (Intimacy!)

As I started to eat, the food multiplied so that we could hardly move in the shop for food. I knew that I had to take this food to everyone outside. Jesus said to me, 'Unless you eat, no one else gets to eat.' I asked Jesus, 'Can we go on a road trip?' He said, 'Yes!' and we went all over Scotland, eating and handing out food.

Unless we eat, no-one else is going to eat.

To be missional, to be purposeful, it all starts with intimacy. So stand up and open the door.

SO:

God has a groove, a rhythm and a pattern for your life. A way of walking that will allow you to be you and to flow with him. Find it. I have found that being intentional about walking with Jesus is the only way that you find and sustain rhythm. If you don't practice this already, why not set aside three spaces in your day to formally encounter Jesus.

- First thing in the morning – start the day with Jesus. Invite him to be Lord, ask the Holy Spirit to lead you and intentionally resolve to live out of your sonship.
- At midday – set an alarm on your phone and allow yourself to be interrupted. Pray the Lord's Prayer reminding yourself of his power and involvement and your need of him.
- Last thing at night – examine your day. What are you happy to leave behind? What do you need to repent for or put right? What do you have to be thankful for and take into a new day?

And just once in a while take a quiet day. A day when you just plan to be with God, say nothing, meet no-one. Walk with Jesus, eat with Jesus, listen to Jesus.

PART 3.

STAND FIRM
STAND FREE

•

Stand firm, and you will win life.
Luke 21:19

WHEN WE STAND UP THERE WILL BE THOSE WHO STAND WITH US. THERE WILL ALSO BE THOSE WHO STAND AGAINST US. AS WE STAND WE WILL BE OPPOSED, UNDERMINED, OPPRESSED. STAND FIRM. ITS THE ONLY WAY IF IDENTITY AND PURPOSE ARE TO BE MATURED IN US. STAND FREE. ITS THE ONLY WAY IF IDENTITY AND PURPOSE ARE TO GROW IN US. FOR WE ARE DESTINED FOR MORE AND WE ARE OPPOSED BY MANY.

7.

ENEMY OF YOUR STATE

Know your enemy and know yourself and you can fight a hundred battles without disaster.

The Art of War, Sun Tzu (6th century BC)

•

Be alert and of sober mind. Your enemy the devil prowls around like a roaring lion looking for someone to devour.

1 Peter 5:8

We are in a battle. The Scriptures leave no room for doubt. It is a dreadful, dark battle. It isn't a battle just against flesh and blood. And it's more than a spiritual skirmish. Check it out.

> *For our struggle is not against flesh and blood, but against the rulers, against the authorities, against the powers of this dark world and against the spiritual forces of evil in the heavenly realms.*
>
> Ephesians 6:12

It is war. A war that has been won, but a war nonetheless. And wars have casualities. The sad truth is that many believers, my friends and yours, get beaten up, trapped, tricked or taken out because they don't properly engage in this war. We are in a battle and we have to learn to stand – to engage it well. We have to learn to engage it wisely. The Bible warns us to 'Be alert and of sober mind' (1 Peter 5). So I want to tell you about spiritual warfare. Sane spiritual warfare. Not to weird you out or to worry you, but to wise you up.

THE TALE OF TWO KINGDOMS

We live in a spiritual world. And we live in a natural world. Both at the same time. It's like picture-in-picture TV. Both worlds are absolutely real. And they are connected.

In the spiritual world there are two powers: two kingdoms, two dominions, two rulers. God and … anti-god. The Bible calls him Satan. Good and evil, light and darkness. Now, you may think that sounds a little medieval, to talk about Satan and darkness and evil. But does it not ring true? Does it not make sense of *all* the stories of our world? Doesn't the story of light and darkness, good and evil, God and Satan make sense of our *Narnias* and our fairytales, our *Lord of the Rings* and our *Star Wars* and all those stories that capture our imaginations and resonate with our hearts. Isn't that why they connect so strongly?

I think these stories resonate because they have a basis in truth. And when you start to look for it, the evidence of the two kingdoms is clear.

I see evidence of the kingdom of God in those who are not ruled by materialism. Those who go deeper with people and community. It's in love for the unlovely. It's in acts of generosity. It's in respect for others. It's in integration: young and old; men and women; different backgrounds, races, languages. And it's characterised by love. Love, love, love. Wherever there is grace and truth, wherever there is wholeness, healing and forgiveness, there is the kingdom of God. We see it and our hearts are made glad, because it looks a little like home.

But we also see the kingdom of anti-God. The dominion of darkness. It opposes all that is of the kingdom of God. Instead of the sharing of resources for the good of all, it calls for gathering and hoarding. It calls for control. It births addictions to shinier, bigger, better toys. It establishes greed.

Instead of community, the dominion of darkness loves isolation and loneliness. It plants that sense of disconnection. It seeks to leave people bereft of God, and their brothers and sisters. It sows distrust because it hates any form of unity. The old distrust the young and think they are rude, disrespectful hoodie-wearing yobs, and the young think the old are rude, legalistic cardigan-wearing snobs! Generations are fractured. Suspicion, rebellion and destruction thrive in the kingdom of the anti-God. It breeds an intrinsic lack of respect for human life. It hates us for being created in the image of God. It establishes acts like abortion as normal and natural human practice. It has no desire to make poverty history.

The dominion of darkness is a kingdom of lies, for Satan is the father of all lies. He loves to whisper lies about our identity – who we are and what we can become. He delights in pedalling lies about our need to look after number one. He nurtures selfishness and self-obsession. He offers lies suggesting God is not there. He loves that notion! He is the subtle inspiration behind a worldview that proclaims there is no absolute truth, that everything is relative.

So there is a clash of kingdoms, of these two powers. And we have a battle. And the battle is real, and the battle is bloody and the battle is a battle for people's hearts, minds and souls and for the hearts, minds and souls of our city and of our nation, and of our world.

BACKSTORY

So where did it all start? We need to know the story or we will never understand the battle that we find ourselves in. The Bible tells us that 'Anti-God', or Satan, is a created being, an angel, in fact an archangel. He was beautiful and powerful: check out Ezekiel 28:13–15.

Then he fell. You'll find that in Isaiah.

> *You said in your heart,*
> *'I will ascend to the heavens;*
> *I will raise my throne*
> *above the stars of God;*
> *I will sit enthroned on the mount of assembly,*
> *on the utmost heights of Mount Zaphon.*
> *I will ascend above the tops of the clouds;*
> *I will make myself like the Most High.'*
> *But you are brought down to the realm of the dead,*
> *to the depths of the pit.*

Isaiah 14:13–15

Satan fell because he wanted to be God. He was desperate to have authority and power. He wanted to sit on the throne of the heavens and of the earth. His sin was that he wanted to be like the Most High. He wanted to be like God. More than that, he wanted to *be* God. In Hebrew the word is *el eloim*, which is translated 'the Most High' and also means 'the possessor of heaven and earth'.

He wanted to be God.

So he was thrown out of heaven. The Lord Jesus was there: '*I saw Satan fall like lightning from heaven*' (Luke 10:18).

In the Garden of Eden, Adam and Eve were given authority by God. Authority to subdue things, to rule over things, to name things, to take care of things. Authority over the fish of the sea and the birds of the air, authority over the garden, over all living things. Humanity was at home with God and God was at home with humanity and humanity was in harmony with creation. And it was paradise.

Satan hated it. Why did he hate it? He hated the relationship we had with God the Father. He also hated the fact that humanity had been given authority. Because that was his idea, that was what *he* wanted. And that was why he was thrown out of heaven.

Satan then comes in the form of a serpent to Adam and Eve. He's not just trying to get Adam and Eve; he's trying to get authority. That is what he really wants. So he twists God's words and Adam and Eve succumb. They place the words of Satan above the words of God and suddenly he's got them. And he's got authority. Jesus himself recognises Satan's authority. In the desert as he is being tempted, Satan offers to give Jesus the kingdoms of this Earth if he worships him. Jesus reacts, but he doesn't rebuke or ridicule Satan for offering something that is not his to give. Satan takes authority and he uses that authority to try to destroy every single work of God. He destroys creation. He destroys relationships: our relationships with people and with God and with ourselves. Satan just goes around destroying things. Even the earth begins to deteriorate. The created order starts spinning out of control, plates move, volcanoes erupt, plagues break out, there is sickness and death. And what is God doing at this time? Well, he's watching. He's got a plan and, in the fullness of time ...

He comes.

The one who creates heaven and earth leaves the throne room of heaven and steps down into his creation. He incarnates himself, he takes on flesh and he moves into the neighbourhood. He comes teaching the kingdom of God and he says, 'there is a different way, there is another rule and that rule is beautiful. And it is here right now'. And he resists Satan for forty days in the desert. Satan says all this stuff to him, all this temptation, and he resists Satan. And he goes around destroying the works of the evil one. And then sets his face towards the cross. And he dies. And just as he does that, on the cross, he says:

'*Tetellestai.*'

'It is finished.' 'It is accomplished'. What is finished? Satan's free reign. Finished! All the things that get busted by Satan get restored at the cross. Jesus dies. He goes down into hell. He taps Satan on the shoulder and he says 'I'll have the keys. I'll have the keys. I'll have the authority.' (My paraphrase. Check out Revelation 1:18.)

Then, on the shore of Lake Galilee he meets the disciples and he says to them:

> '*All authority in heaven and on earth has been given to me. Therefore go and make disciples of all nations, baptising them in the name of the Father and of the Son and of the Holy Spirit, and teaching them to obey everything I have commanded you.*'
>
> Matthew 28:18–20

What he's doing is this: he's giving back to men and to women the authority that they lost under Adam. He's taken it from Satan.

I'll have the keys.

So now you and I have authority. Jesus authority. The kingdom is here. We are free to return to our Father, stand in our sonship, co-operate with Jesus, full of the Holy Spirit.

AFTERMATH

Satan knows his battle has been lost, but he hasn't quite accepted it, hasn't quite got the message yet. He wants his authority back. He's thrashing around and he's taking down as many as he can. And he'll do everything he possibly can to disable you and derail you from living in God's authority and under his power. Which is why you experience pain and opposition and defeat and yo-yo Christianity and two steps forward, one step back.

Jesus has won the victory. It was decided at the cross. Jesus defeated Satan. The victory was signed, sealed and will be delivered. We will celebrate all that this means when Jesus comes again. Jesus will destroy Satan and all his works. The dominion of darkness will be erased, leaving the kingdom of God as all there is. That's the outcome and we can be joyful and confident in that.

So God's kingdom is here, and one day his kingdom will be all there is. But for now it's a hard battle and it's a dark battle. It's a vicious battle and it's a messy battle. And for now we have to fight.

WHERE'S YOUR HEAD AT?

Let's look at some perspectives that it would be *un*helpful to have.

Head under the bed

Some people seem to believe there is a devil under the bed and a devil in the TV, a devil in the cornflakes. 'Here a devil, there a devil, everywhere a devil, devil.' This is a deceit of Satan, to have you terrorised by the idea that there are demons everywhere. You can live your life absolutely paralysed and also justifying everything that you ever do wrong by saying a demon made you do it. When sometimes you are just … naughty. Sometimes bad stuff happens because we make bad choices. And sometimes, stuff just happens. It can be as simple as that. So let's not overestimate Satan's power. He's a lion but he's defeated.

Head in the clouds

Satan sometimes wants to draw us out – but we can get distracted or hurt by trying to deal with things that are too big for us. It would be a mistake to go and stand on hills and scream at territorial spirits, if God hasn't necessarily specifically asked us to do that and we don't have authority to do that. Satan may be an ancient, old, injured, chained lion – but he's still a lion. You don't poke a lion in the eye with a stick and expect to get away with it. So yes, we believe in territorial spirits. Yes, Satan sometimes binds areas. But we need to be very wise in how we deal with these things.

Head in the sand

Probably the most common perspective is that we feel we have got enough problems with sin in our lives and relationships that are going wrong so we don't need to know about Satan and his demons. So we stick our fingers in our ears and sing '*la la la la* ...' It all seems like whacky medieval Tolkein stuff and we don't really want to think about it and everything's a coincidence. Satan loves that because when you deny he's got power he can just mess with your life. At best you will live your life with your head in the sand and at worst he will suffocate the passion for the God life out of you.

This battle is all around us, and yet so often we fail to get what is going on. Satan's tactic is to hide in the shadows. His power comes from staying unseen, lest we should run to the Living God. The demonic rarely looks like it does on TV. If a child's head spins and speaks with the voice of James Earl Jones, Satan has pretty much blown his cover. Satan does not often do obvious. The demonic works subtly, and has us thinking things and behaving in ways that are anti-God. His lies seem sensible, justified, and rational. They undermine the breaking through of the kingdom of God. The lies undermine it, but they can't destroy it.

Many Christians are walking around in unbelief. They are struggling with faith, even those who completely believe. They are largely disarmed in life, simply because they have not been wary of the enemy's cunning devices.

FIRST PRINCIPLES

The end goal is unambiguous: Satan wants to take you out. His intent is to destroy the work of God in your life by any means possible. So how do we approach this battle?

God wants you free and healthy, alive and fruitful. I want that for you and you want that for you. So we are all in agreement. But let me help you with a simple four-fold battle plan for sane spiritual warfare designed to move beyond agreement towards freedom and fruitfulness. I am tempted to go further still. If you adopt this plan you will begin to see changes. You will find yourself able in a new way to appropriate your identity and see breakthrough that, at the moment, you struggle to believe for.

- Face the Father
- Dress for battle
- Get military intelligence
- Go on the offensive.

The first two points to this plan we will discuss in this chapter and the final two will be unpacked in the next.

FACE THE FATHER

You don't engage in sane spiritual warfare by facing the devil. You face the Father. Some Christians seem to have more faith in the devil than they have in the Father. They spend more time worrying about the enemy and what he's going to do than they spend basking in the love that the Father has for us. Instead you need to get to know who Father God is, get to know how capable *he* is, get to know how powerful *he* is, get to understand what it means to have sonship and to operate out of oneness with him. If you still aren't really sure who God is, and what he is like, go back and read chapter three again. Get to know what it means to operate out of oneness, the power that you have in you. Face the Father. The battle belongs to the Lord – not to you.

DRESS FOR BATTLE

Read Ephesians 6.

The Belt of Truth

The first piece of armour isn't actually armour at all – but it is essential. In fact it's so essential that if you didn't have it on, you would either end up naked, or your tunic would get in the way so much that you would not be able to fight. Your belt enables you to gird up your loins, literally. It prepares you for action. With the belt in place, you are ready for war. So what is the belt of truth? Two things are implied:

1. *The truth of who Jesus is.* There is no way you will be in any fit state to engage the battle unless you are confident and standing on the truth of who Jesus is, what he has done and that you are secure in Him. Your stand will be fatally flawed if you rely on what and how you feel. Do you believe in God? Do you believe in Jesus? Do you believe he came and died and rose again? Do you believe? I don't mean 'Is it rational?' Or, 'Can you prove it?' I mean, 'Do you believe it in your heart?' The Greek word translated 'faith' which we find all over the New Testament is the word *pisteo*. Its literal meaning is to step out in faith. Believing then is about practically basing the weight of your life, your future, your walking . . . and everything on what you understand to be the truth. Stand on it!

2. *Integrity.* Be in no doubt: God is calling the believer in any age, and particularly today, to a life of truth and integrity. The number one turn-off for non-believers is Christians who

don't walk the way they talk. Put on truth, walk as you are called to walk so that others can recognise it as truth. If, for example, we believe God is love and we are supposed to put our weight on that belief, then people all around us are supposed to see the love flowing from our actions.

The Breastplate of Righteousness

In ancient times the breastplate was made just the right size and shape to cover and protect all the vital organs. The breastplate protects your heart. Your heart is precious. Paul says in Romans 10 that it is with your heart you believe. It's where belief stems from.

Our hearts can get damaged. They get damaged by ungodly expectations. They get damaged by negative words spoken over us. They get damaged by love ungiven.

This much is certain – we are going to take flak in life. People will say and do things against us. There are times when people are going to use and abuse us. They will upset us and mistreat us. That is life. It is a reflection of the fallen, messed up world we live in. Our hearts are vulnerable. We desperately need the breastplate of righteousness. It enables us to walk in an opposite spirit. It enables us to walk in wholeness.

His breastplate not only protects our vulnerable hearts but also, in covering us, it has the ability to justify us, to set us right to vindicate us and to restore and heal us? Yes! So put the breastplate on. *Father I choose to let you defend me, to let you be my judge. Restore me and protect me, Father, please.*

The boots of the Gospel of peace

In Paul's day soldiers' boots were leather and studded. They enabled soldiers to march long and hard. They prevented their feet from slipping. They marched phenomenal distances, twenty-five miles in a day, fifty if forced. They marched on roads they had built. For a world that walked most places, good boots were very important.

There is always a danger of falling in battle. We all know people who have slipped, people who have lost their faith. But God has made provision for each of us to stand. How do you stand? You move in the opposite spirit. You don't run. You step out with the Gospel of peace. Peace with others. Peace with God. A ready offense is a great strategy for defence. As ludicrous as this may sound – pressing further into relationship with God will not only bring on full-scale attack, it is also your best form of divine defence.

The enemy hates the Gospel of peace because it saves the lost and it brings people into a relationship with Jesus. It turns darkness into light.

Shield of Faith

A Roman shield was over a metre long. It completely covered the whole body. It was often used against arrows, which were dipped in pitch, lit and then fired. It was efficient, and highly effective.

If you stand in truth and you live holy, live right and you love, if you step out in the truth, you are engaging the battle and you become fair game. Satan's arrows will come. Arrows of fear. Arrows of guilt. They'll tell you: 'You can not stand;' 'Look at what you have done;' 'You can never be forgiven.' 'Your faith is has no basis in reason.' They'll hit you where you feel most vulnerable.

But we have Father God's protection. Take up the shield of faith! Understand the limits of knowledge and the many academic gurus who have been wrong. Don't give up meeting together because it's in the together that we can best be reminded of the truth, even when it doesn't feel like truth and many ridicule it. Submit your mind to the authority of the Scriptures. Never allow the revelation of Scripture to be lowered by your personal experience.

The gift of the mind – of apprehension and of understanding – is one of the greatest gifts Father God has given to us. But our minds are an obvious target for Satan. If Christ's gift is the transformation of a renewed mind and supernatural power results, then Satan's strategy has been to take captive that mind. The enemy uses two particular tactics, amongst others –

1. He will use any philosophy to debunk the credibility of God's truth – postmodernity, or modernity, or higher criticism. Paul's response was 'I resolved to know nothing, but Christ and him crucified'.

2. He will convince you that it is all about knowledge, and that any experience is secondary and emotional. By his approach, you end up knowing the book, but not the author.

How do we counter these tactics? Once again we walk in the opposite spirit and we say, 'Come Holy Spirit. You are the Spirit of truth.' (This is particularly important for those of you doing theology degrees in secular institutions.) 'Come Holy Spirit, be my shield of faith.' Satan may retort, 'You have never *really* experienced life in all fullness, you don't know victory and fruitfulness.' But call on the Spirit. He will come. He is undeniable. He reminds us of what has been accomplished for us. Know this, and be assured of this: everyone who calls on the name of the Lord will be saved. The wages of sin is death, but the gift of God is abundant life, and life in all its fullness. 'If you declare with your mouth, "Jesus is Lord," and believe in your heart that God raised him from the dead, you will be saved' (Romans 10:9). So do not be worried, or upset. He will lose none of those given to him. Satan wants us to be unsure and ineffective. Just allow the Holy Spirit, on a regular basis, to speak over you the truth of your salvation.

The Sword of the Spirit

The Greek word *rhema*, is 'the utterance of God'. It has cutting power. This is what Jesus stood on when the devil came to him in the wilderness. It's what God has spoken. This is how a man, or woman, will keep their ways pure. This is how we can advance. Here are words of life. Show me any passionate, devoted and fruitful believer, and I will show you a person devoted to the Word of God. I will show you a person who lives the Word daily.

How do you advance? You pray! You pray the word of God. If this battle is spiritual then we must engage spiritual means, in order to have any opportunity to win.

We stand. We wait on God. We pray. Every single renewal and revival in the church started when people got serious about prayer. We pray as we breathe. We pray 24-7 and we pray accountably, in small groups. We make prayer second nature – a continual dialogue with Father God.

In the community of the early church there is a story that powerfully reminds us of the importance of prayer. You will find it in Acts 12. The church is under attack. James has been beheaded and Peter has been imprisoned. The church gathers to pray. By the end of the chapter, Peter has been miraculously released, Herod is dead and the church is growing. If you want to see breakthrough and victory you must learn to pray.

The Helmet of Salvation

The Roman helmet, or 'Galea', was made of bronze or iron. It often had plumes on top to make the soldier seem taller – but more importantly it helped identify who he represented – which legion – and the authority that he carried.

Put on the helmet of salvation. Remind your earthly distracted self of your standing and identity in Christ. You are a son of the Father, one with Jesus and full of the Holy Spirit. Satan is a pretty formidable foe. But so are you. Remember you carry the authority of Jesus as you are sent to represent him in this battle.

This is as useful in battle offensive as it is in protection. There have been a number of occasions when praying for someone who is experiencing severe demonic attack that I have addressed the demon directly. 'My name is Karl. I am a son of God. I am one with Jesus Christ and I represent him. I am full of the power of the Holy Spirit and I instruct you to be gone. *Now.*

Put on your helmet.

———————————————— SO: ————————————————

Read Ephesians 6 and pray on the armour of God: do it for yourself, for family and friends. Apparently (depending on which psychologists you read and which ones you believe) it takes between 3–5 months to form a habit! Start with a week; pray the armour on every morning. Remember we are in a war!

8.

MILITARY INTELLIGENCE

'*Victorious Warriors win first and then go to war, while defeated warriors go to war first then seek to win.*'
The Art of War, Sun Tzu (6th century BC)

•

'*For though we live in the world, we do not wage war as the world does. The weapons we fight with are not the weapons of the world. On the contrary, they have divine power to demolish strongholds. We demolish arguments and every pretension that sets itself up against the knowledge of God, and we take captive every thought to make it obedient to Christ.*'
2 Corinthians 10:3–5

am built for fighting rather than running. However in my best moments I do occasionally jog. Usually at dusk so as not to frighten small children and animals. But recently I was out running in the light. My iPod was turned right up – usually nobody is around – and I was belting out at the top of my not inconsiderable lungs 'Wohh-oh oh-oh. I'm not backing down. I will stand my ground. Lifting high the name of Jesus.' (IMHO one of the very best war cry songs out there.) I was doing it proud at a stadium praise volume. I opened my mouth to go for it again, and as I did so suddenly realised that gawping at me as if to say, 'What is that thing? What is that noise?' was a whole busload of school rugby teams.

Contemporary Christian worship music has gone through a number of distinctive genres recently. We have sung the psalms to folksy tunes, we have done 'rounds' where you never quite knew where you were supposed to come in or stop and for a time we had a neo-Hebraic obsession – the Christian grapevine dance with a 'Hoy!' at the end of each chorus. We marched for Jesus, and 'made way' for him. We went through a 'dance, dance' phase, perhaps a hangover from liturgical dance groups with unredeemed public lycra: 'I have a hamster – would you like to see my hamster?' 'I roll the duvet – I unroll the duvet!' All the while most of my (mainly white, middle class) congregation would look deadly embarrassed and couldn't wait to sit down.

We used to sing about binding the devil: 'Smash him, bash him, bind him up, crush him.' But we don't sing songs like this anymore. Now, musically at least, we might be better off than we once were. But spiritually we are possibly less prepared, less framed and less able to engage the spiritual battle that is waged against us.

We have an enemy. And he doesn't fight fair. He knows us and he knows our weaknesses. And he has a quiver of tactics at hand to use against us.

And as military strategists will tell you, victory is generally won by those who know and understand the moves of their enemy. So it is essential that we take a look at *his* moves.

UNDER THE INFLUENCE

Paul describes how we used to be bound by the ways of this world, enslaved by the cravings of our own flesh, and ultimately by the enemy of God, 'the ruler of the kingdom of the air, the spirit who is now at work in those who are disobedient' (Ephesians 2:2). Then he explains that God in his mercy and grace set us free. He saved us. We have been saved by grace. We're saved to do good works. We're saved to express grace towards other people. We're saved to be like Christ and act like Christ.

But the enemy, the anti-God, hates this. He hates us understanding who we are, he hates us living the life we were meant to live. So he will do his best to mislead us. He can't win us, but he can wound us. He can take us out of the battle. That's why we who are forgiven don't always experience that forgiveness – we don't feel or really believe we are forgiven. It's why we who are sons of God often don't fully realise that we are. We end up living as orphans. We live as if we have to compete for God's approval, as if we have to earn his love.

We have to appropriate our freedom. We are, positionally and legally, free. We are saved. And yet we live as if we are still bound, still guilty for something we did or said years ago, still ruled by an addiction to alcohol or anger. We still follow the ways of this world, 'the lust of the flesh, the lust of the eyes, and the pride of life' (1 John 2:16). This behaviour does not come from the Father, does not look like the Son and is not inspired by the Spirit. How can this happen?

Can a Christian be influenced by Satan? Yes.

Can a Christian be demon-possessed? No.

The word that is sometimes translated 'demon possession' in the New Testament is *daimonizomai* (Mark 1:32, Matthew 8:28). It is an unfortunate translation. The phrase 'under demonic influence' or 'demonised' would be more accurate, describing a person living to a greater or lesser degree under demonic influence. Is that possible? Is it biblical? For someone to be a follower of God, to belong to Jesus Christ and to be influenced by Satan? Yes. Think about it. Jesus speaks to Peter and says 'get behind me Satan'. Who's he talking to? He's talking to Satan. In Acts 5, Ananias and Sapphira demonstrated that it is possible to be a follower of Jesus and to allow Satan to fill your heart. In the Old Testament, the story of Job describes in detail someone who believed in God, and was devout and a follower of God, and Satan was given permission to mess with him. And when Paul writes, he writes to believers, to the church. So Ephesians 4:26–31 shows it is possible *not* to fully put off the old self, and for bitterness, rage and anger, brawling and slander, and other non-Jesus living still to evidence itself in the life of believers.

FOOTHOLDS

So, writing to these Ephesian believers, believers who have received Jesus, who have had their sin forgiven and are walking in the light of Jesus, believers that he lived with and taught for three years, Paul suggests that when we act in a way that is inconsistent with the grace we have received, we give permission for Satan to have a negative impact or influence on our lives.

> 'In your anger do not sin': do not let the sun go down while you are still angry, and do not give the devil a foothold. Anyone who has been stealing must steal no longer, but must work, doing something useful with their own hands, that they may have something to share with those in need.
>
> Do not let any unwholesome talk come out of your mouths, but only what is helpful for building others up according to their needs, that it may benefit those who listen. And do not grieve the Holy Spirit of God, with whom you were sealed for the day of redemption. Get rid of all bitterness, rage and anger, brawling and slander, along with every form of malice. Be kind and compassionate to one another, forgiving each other, just as in Christ God forgave you.'
>
> Ephesians 4:26–32

The word translated 'foothold' is the Greek word *topos*. We get the word topography from it. It means a place where a ruler governs, a place of jurisdiction. Don't let anger fester in you, says Paul, or you may give the enemy territory in your life.

What does this do? It's a bit like giving Satan a permission slip to mess with your life. It allows him the opportunity to ensnare you. Here are some examples where Scripture specifically says believers may give Satan access to their lives.

- Continuing to live out of anger and bitterness, indulging in unwholesome talk, stealing (Ephesians 4:26–28).
- Opposing God's truth, refusing to accept the authority of the word of God (2 Timothy 2).
- Being greedy, hypocritical, lying (Acts 5:1–10).
- Refusing to forgive (2 Corinthians 2:10, 11).
- Being covetous, materialistic (1 Timothy 6:9).
- Living with a religious spirit, the spirit of the Pharisees (2 Corinthians 11:3, 4).

Don't allow yourself to act in a way that is not consistent with the grace you have received in Jesus. Don't steal. Don't indulge in gossip or criticism or lies. Don't give in to anger or bitterness or any kind of malice. Don't respond out of competitiveness or jealousy or unforgiveness. All of these grow and flourish on the enemy's land. They find their home on his turf. Each time you give in to one of them, it becomes more natural, more difficult to resist the next time. Gradually it becomes part of your character, and you give Satan open access to mess with you. Live with these in your life and you give him a foothold!

If you are deliberately and consistently disobedient to God's word, if you decide to read the Bible according to the way you want to read the Bible rather than according to the way the Bible is written. If you sin and don't repent, and continue in sin. If you do this, not only can you expect not to be blessed, you can expect to be attacked as well. And that foothold, if you don't deal with it, can begin to suffocate the God-life and prevent you standing up and standing free. More than simply a place of jurisdiction, it can be a base of operations, a wrong way of thinking, and one that will keep you bound.

STRONGHOLDS

So we need to go on the offensive. We do not need to be scared of what Satan is doing. We have the authority and the means to dismantle the strongholds that keep us bound and keep us from the deeper things of God.

> *For though we live in the world, we do not wage war as the world does. The weapons we fight with are not the weapons of the world. On the contrary, they have divine power to demolish strongholds. We demolish arguments and every pretension that sets itself up against the knowledge of God, and we take captive every thought to make it obedient to Christ.*
>
> 2 Corinthians 10:3–5 (NIV 1984)

That word translated 'stronghold' or 'fortress' here is the Greek word *ochuroma*. A base of operations, for Satan's work of deception, for his work of ruin, destruction and death. Here's my definition:

> *A spiritual stronghold is a pattern or system of warped thinking according to God and his truths. It allows, or influences, wrong perceptions, behaviour and actions. It deeply affects the way we relate to God, ourselves and the people around us.*

So, we come to know Christ by grace. We are saved, but unless we deal with our past properly, we bring baggage with us. We get forgiven, yet we still have patterns of thinking and living and experiences to work through, as we work out our salvation and learn what it is to live as sons. All the things that we did are forgiven, but we still need to learn new ways of thinking and new ways of living. We need to have our minds and hearts and lives renewed. If the old ways and beliefs linger, they can cause spiritual damage. This has the capacity to rob us of the life God has for each one of us. And it has serious implications for our missional potential.

Here are some examples:

- You were involved in an unhelpful relationship that has damaged the way you think and feel and your ability to build healthy relationships now. Perhaps you have no model or pattern for a healthy relationship.
- You had an addiction to pornography, which meant you viewed others as objects, in a way that is wrong.
- You had an unhealthy misuse of money.
- You had alcohol or drug or food addictions, and a habit of seeking solace in these.
- Perhaps you dabbled in the occult. Ouija boards, tarot cards, psychic readings other religions, Freemasonry. You need to shut those doors.

The world tells us that there is nothing wrong with many of these things, the enemy offers a subtle encouragement to explore sexuality and sensuality, to enjoy more food than we need, to buy more than we need, spend more on what is shinier and newer. We all find ourselves powerfully influenced by worldviews that seem perfectly reasonable and are so easily imbibed but are at odds with the kingdom of God. The resultant individualism, materialism, pluralism, humanism and hedonism have eventually killed us like a long, slow, cumulative poison.

Don't you want to be free of those patterns of behaviour that continue to occur in your life? Don't you want to be free of those strongholds? Don't you want to walk in freedom with your heavenly Father? The good news is, that we can be. We have the resources to deal with these things. Weapons with 'divine power to demolish strongholds'.

First, we need to submit ourselves to God. We need to repent, rebuke the enemy, allow God to renew us and receive the Holy Spirit.

*Submit yourselves, then, to God. Resist the devil, and he will flee
from you. Come near to God and he will come near to you. Wash
your hands …*

James 4:7

Repent

Submit yourself to God in repentance. Ask Father God to
make clear any patterns of wrong thinking that are damaging
you and others. And ask forgiveness for your sin, rebellion,
unwholesome talk, or critical anger or judgemental heart.
Repent is the Greek word *metanoia*. It means to change
your mind, to ask forgiveness and to walk in the opposite spirit.

Rebuke

Resist Satan and he will flee from you. Some guys do the most
fruit-looped things, shout at the devil and scream at him and
bind everything in sight and all that jazz. I'm not asking you to
do that. But it is crucial, according to Scripture, that we confront
Satan. He's not God. In comparison to God he is an itsy bitsy
devil. But he needs confronting. Jesus came to destroy the works
of the evil one (1 John 3:8) and he passed that on to us as a
mandate. If that is our job and that is our calling, we had better
start with our own lives. Part of the reason that we do not stand,
that we take one step forward, one step back, part of the reason
we walk around with a limp – is that we are attempting to pursue
righteousness without resisting Satan. It's time that we had a toe-
to-toe confrontation with the enemy. Look him in the eye and
rebuke him in the name of Jesus. Because of what Jesus has done
on the cross, because of his blood.

How? You just tell him. Something like this. 'Every
stronghold that you have constructed I tear down in the name
of Jesus. I take captive every thought and I bring them to the
cross. I am a child of the Father; I am a son of the living God.
My life is now hidden with Christ in God. I am filled with the
Holy Spirit of Jesus and I choose this day to tear down the

stronghold of individualism and consumerism, of guilt and fear and love deprivation and a critical spirit and jealousy and the fear of man and freemasonry and greed and religious spirits and abuse and pornography and sexual promiscuity and lying and cheating and greed and materialism … (Add your stuff.) Be gone. You have no authority. Be gone.'

Renew

Draw near to God and he will draw near to you. He is the divine rebuilder of ancient ruins; he is the restorer of streets without dwellings. He wants to give you back the years the locusts have eaten. He is the perfect forgiver, he is the wonderful Father, he delights in you, and he wants to give you good things. So when you repent, when you have rebuked Satan, ask the Lord to renew you. Ask him to give you back the energy and power that has been missing. Dare to ask him to bless you in areas you have known lack. Ask for a divine exchange: your fear for his courage, your pain for his healing, your insecurity for his security. Go on.

Receive

Then you just ask the Holy Spirit to fill you. Take a moment to be quiet, and just say 'Holy Spirit, would you come.' And wait for him to come. He will. Brilliant!

Wouldn't it be great if I could now tell you 'it's all done, you need never concern yourself with the enemy again, he won't come near anymore'. I'm sorry. Yes the battle has been engaged and the victory is around. But the fight still rages.

THE ULTIMATE CASE STUDY IN ATTACK.

Jesus allows us an eyewitness perspective on how all this works in his encounter with Satan in the desert. It's magnificent and sobering but it's there to prepare us for what is coming our way.

(I am completely indebted to Mike Breen for his work here, from *Multiplying Missional Leaders* 3DM 2012.)

Jesus has been baptised in the river Jordan by his cousin John. The heavens open and a dove descends upon him, the gift of the Holy Spirit, and a voice comes from heaven: 'This is my Son, whom I love; with him I am well pleased' (Matthew 3:17). We are witnessing the high point of his commissioning, his identity is clear. Immediately Jesus is led by the Holy Spirit into the wilderness to be tempted by Satan.

And Satan's strategy is to question that identity: *If* you are the Son of God. Satan knows if he can undermine the identity of Jesus, the ball game is over. If he can get Jesus believing perhaps he isn't and perhaps he's not going to, then it is all over for Jesus, for salvation history. This is Satan's key tactic. It is still his key tactic with us.

There are three ways that Satan attacks Jesus' identity. And I guarantee that you will find you experience one of them, if not all three. Because these are archetypal temptations, Satan's best tactics. You can be sure that if he used this strategy against Jesus, the Son of God, he's going to use it at some point against you.

Appetite

First is appetite, 'tell these stones to become bread' (Matthew 4:3). It seems an innocent suggestion. You can imagine that whisper, 'You've been forty days without eating? You're a hungry guy and you've got a lot of things to do and you need your strength. Really, does God make you do this kind of thing? I mean, *really?*'

But what is really being questioned is Jesus sonship, his relationship with his father. In essence, '*If* you're the Son of God.' Are you really the Son of God? Are you *really* a child of God? Will your heavenly Father *really* provide for you and give you the things that you need to get through this life and to enjoy life? The temptation is to gratify an immediate desire, and consequently to forfeit a real long-term dependence on our heavenly Father.

Appetite is like a child craving attention. It will come at you and come at you. And the more you give into it the more it comes at you, again and again. It cries 'feed me'. TV is not a bad thing. Sex is not a bad thing; it's a good thing. Food is not a bad thing; it's a good thing. Exercise is not a bad thing; it's a good thing. All these are good things. But if the enemy can convince you they are the things you *need*, and you begin to meet your own needs, and your meeting your own needs becomes your focus, you deny that opportunity for the Father to care for you and provide for you. You stop trusting him. Perhaps you find that your needs are not met and suddenly you need to store up more and more and more of these things and you find it is out of control. You are addicted to these things, you need them first and foremost, and your heavenly Father's provision is just an optional extra.

Jesus' response says, 'I trust that God is my Father, that he is a good dad. He will take care of me, he will give me good things in a good way.' This is really counter-intuitive, it is hard for us to get our heads around. Because the philosophy of this world is 'You need to look after number one'. It's incredibly selfish. It's also 'if it feels good, do it. It doesn't hurt anyone else, go and enjoy it, grab at it, have it, why shouldn't you? You deserve it'. The enemy is always chipping away, whispering: 'You're going to miss out, you're not going to have life in all its fullness, you're not going to have abundance.' But the more you have the less it satisfies. And instead of rejecting it and running to the Father, you just want more. And before you know it you are bound to an appetite addiction.

But the philosophy of the kingdom of God is to seek first the kingdom of God and all his righteousness, and all this other stuff gets added unto you. The philosophy of the kingdom of God is that the fruit of the Spirit is love, joy, peace, patience, and self-control. It comes from the spirit of God. Self control. Jesus says the way to live in step with him starts with denying self (Luke 9:23), so fast from the things you can, and ask God to help you loosen the addiction to the things you can't. You are not defined by your addiction. You do not need to be controlled by your addiction. It does not need to be an addiction. Face the Father.

Ambition

Satan's second tactic is ambition. He showed Jesus all the kingdoms of the world and said, 'I will give you all their authority and splendour; it has been given to me, and I can give it to anyone I want to. If you worship me, it will all be yours' (Luke 4:6, 7).

Some of us have an ambition addiction. An addiction to success or winning. Winning is not wrong. Winning is OK. But if your identity is dependent on winning or losing, on whether you get certain qualifications, on whether you get promoted at work, on the particular path your career takes, *that* is a problem. The philosophy of this world is that you are your skills and your successes. You are what you can do and what you achieve. It is driven into us. It is a piece of nonsense.

The Bible is full of weird upside-down stuff like . . . 'my power is made perfect in weakness' (2 Corinthians 12:9). How does that work? It is almost offensive in our society.

So Satan offers Jesus all authority and splendour, incredible success, incredible global success. (And notice that when Satan says they are his to give, Jesus doesn't say they are not.) There would be no need to serve a broken world, no touching lepers, no rejection from Pharisees, no scourging, no whipping, nobody abusing him, no cross. That could be tempting. Very tempting.

God's path of power and authority leads to a cross. But it changes the world.

When we are bound by ambition, we become driven and busy and goal-orientated, and striving and people-using. We work so hard. And we compare ourselves to others; we are judging people all the time, as to whether they are winners or losers, failures or successes.

But according to the kingdom of God that criteria is absolute rubbish.

I'm sick of it personally, sick of the 'skills + hard work = success' formula. It works a bit, but it's so limited. And if the salvation of our city and our nation is dependent on my skills and my successes, on your skills and your successes, there's no hope. There's no hope for 98% of our city who don't know Jesus, no matter how hard we try with our bridge diagrams and our house-to-house evangelism or whatever slicker contemporary versions of it we dream up. There's no hope. What we need is the cross. And resurrection.

I put my hand up here. I've grown up wanting to be successful, to plant hundreds of churches and in my best moments it's all for the glory of God, but in my worst moments it's about skills and success. And when I see people doing things I want to do I find myself getting jealous of what God is doing with them. And if I let it stay there it creates this root of bitterness in me, and if I don't get that dug out, it prevents me from walking in the deeper things of God. I want resurrection. So bring on the cross. Bring on the cross. All the stuff in me that is incompatible with Christ in me, that is incompatible with my identity in him – his way – I want to be cut off and thrown into the fire, however painful that may be. Because I want to see resurrection.

So how do we position ourselves? How do we train our hearts in the way of the cross? We need to learn to choose to lose. What would that look like? What would it look like if we decided not to have the last word in an argument, if we were to let someone else have it? What would it look like if we were to play to play rather than playing to win? What would it look like if we chose to work for a bigger reality than us, and we decided it really didn't matter who got the credit for it, no matter who did what? What would it look like if we chose faithfulness to the thing we've been asked to do, even if it is not the thing we really want to do? And we did it really well, rather than spending our lives dreaming of the thing we always wanted to do. If I just got faithful to God in my corner doing what God asked me to do, accepting that if he promotes me, he promotes me, because that's his business. What would that look like?

It would look like the cross. The resurrection.

If you're an ambition addict, 'Humble yourselves before the Lord, and he will lift you up' (James 4:10). Do you believe that your Father has the best for you, has good things for you? There is no better plan for your life.

Approval

The third temptation is to look for approval. Jesus is taken to the temple, probably the royal porch, the southeast corner of the temple, where there is a cliff that drops away down into the Kidron Valley, 450 feet below. So this is dramatic stuff. Satan says 'If you are the Son of God, ... throw yourself down from here' (Luke 4:9) as if to say, 'It would be really cool, Jesus: you throw yourself down, angels will come, swooping down, everyone's going to see, and they'll know you really are the Messiah. It will really affirm you.'

The approval of others feels good. But if you become dependent upon what you think everyone else thinks of you then it is a problem. Satan says 'Prove it'. And we might not be throwing ourselves off buildings or cliffs but how many times have we sought the approval of others – because affirmation feels great? And although we know that there is a God in heaven who approves of us and loves us and thinks we are fantastic, we still run around looking for approval from the people we know who will say the right things that will give us the right buzz that will get us back on our feet and get us on our way. 'Cos we are approval junkies. And we need them to fill up the well. Do people think I am a good husband, a good wife, a good parent? Do people think I'm smart? Do people think I dress nicely? Do people like me? Am I popular? What are people going to think when I have finished my sermon tonight? The tempter will use the addictive process of affirmation to cripple us. We live in and out of this.

I didn't think this was an issue for me until four years ago – you can live a long time and think you're OK with yourself.

I knew it was an issue when I was a kid. I found myself even lying to people, exaggerating, to build myself up.

Soon after my father died, I was at a conference. Someone I'd never met, gave me a note. It said 'Miss your dad. Grieve for your dad. But live for your heavenly Dad.'

It got me.

Because I realised for the first time that I was an approval addict. I lived, in many ways, for the approval of my dad. I loved my dad. And he was my hero. I would often ring him up and say 'I'm doing this, what do you think?' and I lived in the shadow of that approval. I still struggle a little, but now, I don't care what people think, in all the right ways I don't care what they think. I care what Father God thinks. And I know he thinks I'm brilliant – he thinks I'm great. But I still battle. Every Sunday, without fail, before I stand up and preach I hear this whisper '*Why are you bothering*?' And when I get down I hear '*I told you so*'. Of course we like it when someone says 'You're doing a great job'. But the temptation is to be addicted to that kind of approval.

How do I deal with that? I deal with it exactly the way Jesus dealt with it. In Luke 4, verse 4, verse 8, verse 10 and verse 12, Jesus says '*It is written …*' What I hear in my ear that is contradictory to what God has said is a lie from the pit, and I am going to kill it dead. God has said: 'You did not choose me, but I chose you and appointed you so that you might go and bear fruit' (John 15:16). That was said prophetically over my life, it was my baptismal text; I will repeat it to myself on a daily basis. God has said 'the one who is in you is greater than the one who is in the world' (1 John 4:4). There is nothing to be afraid of. You have all the power. God has said you are 'fearfully and wonderfully made' (Psalm 139:14). Who gets off telling you whether you are good or not, whether you are beautiful or not: you are beautiful, you are a son of the most high God. God has said.

He has said this stuff. It is not that you need to stop hanging around people who give you affirmation. But you need to hang around him who will give you perfect affirmation *more*. That you might have strength and power and authority. That's what you need to hear. Jesus needed to hear it twice at least. At his baptism and at the transfiguration. If Jesus needs to hear this stuff, you need to hear this stuff. You are fearfully and wonderfully made, know that.

Then, Satan leaves until an opportune time.

Power of the Spirit

Jesus returns in the power of the Spirit and goes off immediately out of this moment of victory and he stands up in the synagogue with the Scriptures open. He reads Isaiah 61:

> *... he has anointed me*
> *to proclaim good news to the poor.*
> *He has sent me to proclaim freedom for the prisoners*
> *and recovery of sight for the blind ...*
>
> Luke 4:18

COME ON! I have all the power of my Father, I'm full of the Holy Spirit, I have resisted the enemy and NOW we are about the business of the kingdom of God. The kingdom is here!

Every single time your identity is threatened, every time you face temptation, it is a huge opportunity for the breakthrough of the kingdom of God. Every single time you feel tempted to give in to one of these addictions, every single time it is a huge opportunity for breakthrough in the kingdom, that the devil will flee from you, and that you might walk in righteousness and truth and power.

An opportune time

The tempter will come back again and he will almost certainly come back around your primary temptations. He's not got any new tricks. Your weaknesses will remain your weaknesses. I'm still going to have some weaknesses, perhaps around seeking approval, around ambition. And every single time Satan is going to whisper in my ear. As he did with Jesus. 'I mean, really – you are the Son of God. Do you really have to go to the cross? I mean, truly? Is he really going to make you do that?' And my response will be, 'Not my will, but yours be done.'

But every single time he comes again and he whispers again and he prompts you again, it is just a reminder that the battle has been won – the skirmishes may come, but the battle has been won, because he went to the cross. Your affirmation comes from the Father. Because you sought first the kingdom of God and his righteousness and everything else gets added – and the skirmishes will come. But the battle is won.

SO:

What is your battle? I know you have many, but what is your primary battle? How are you going to walk in the opposite spirit of the disaster that will befall you if you continue to give in to the temptation of the enemy? Make a plan, account for it to someone else and then act.

Go on … Read on …

9.

MOTHER MUGGER

'When you forgive, you love. And when you love, God's light shines upon you.'

Into the Wild, John Krakauer (1996)

●

'Always forgive your enemies; nothing annoys them so much.'

Oscar Wilde (1854–1900)

●

If you O Lord, kept a record of sins, O Lord, who could stand.

Psalm 130:3

ncredible things were happening. Blind people were seeing, lame people were walking, and people were learning about God from a man who talked as if he actually knew him. Something was happening and everyone wanted to be around Jesus.

Mark 2. Jesus travelled to Capernaum, just north of his home town. And everyone wanted to be there. Jesus was big news. You know, centre spread, pull-out section, back page news, front page news. He was the man to be around. Maybe a healing would happen. Maybe he would do something that they could tell their grandkids. 'I was there when Jesus did a healing.' And so the house is stuffed full, it is just rammed.

RAISING THE ROOF

There are four guys who have decided. 'OK, we're going to do this. We are going to get our crippled friend to Jesus. Because Jesus is healing people and maybe he's going to walk again.' And so they take him, four of them carrying him on a stretcher. But the house is rammed. There is no way into the house and everyone is 'Shhh-ing'. Jesus is speaking. So they decide, 'Here's the plan – we'll go up the steps, up onto the roof, and we'll dig into the roof.' And when you hear that you think 'What?' because you live somewhere where the roofs are slate or tiles or somehow solid. And you don't dig through solid roofs. But in Jesus' day the houses had steps up the side and the roof would be made of sticks and mud and palm fronds and it would get damaged. Every year they would replace the roof. And so to dig through the roof wasn't such a stupid idea.

They took the guy up on the roof and they started to dig. Jesus is teaching downstairs. They hear some scratching. Mud and sticks start falling. A hole appears. And some people stop listening to Jesus. And it gets brighter and the sun starts streaming through and then there is someone being lowered through and now no-one is listening to Jesus. It's a comical moment, because there is a guy being lowered through the roof on a stretcher. And, if you are allowed to think these things, I reckon maybe Jesus laughed. This was awkward and ridiculous and pregnant with possibility. This guy who is hoping to get healed is eyeball to eyeball with the Saviour of the world.

I think maybe, possibly, Jesus laughed.

And then Jesus chooses this moment to shine the blinding light of his truth into everyone that is there. And he says to this guy: 'Son, your sins are forgiven' (Mark 2:5).

There is this audible 'Huh?' around the room. A shock, and maybe offence. This is not what the guy came for. This is not what anyone else came to hear and see. They have come to see a healing – to hear great teaching at least. Some of them have come a long way. As soon as they see this guy coming through the roof and that he's crippled they *know* clearly a healing is going to happen. They are imagining telling their grandkids they were there when Jesus did a healing. And maybe some are wanting healing themselves and thinking they could get healed too in the aftermath of this miracle.

But no. The healing that had seemed to be about to happen … doesn't. This guy came, wanting to get healed, he had never even walked and Jesus is calling him a sinner. So actually, this was offensive.

There's another group of people in the room. They are the religious leaders. And they are not just astonished, they are absolutely mind-fried. They can't understand it. They know how difficult it is to forgive sin. They follow and have developed upon scriptural laws. They know that if you do something wrong you have to go to Jerusalem and pick up a lamb and you have to queue up and cut the neck of the lamb and then for a little while you are forgiven of your sin. But then you sin again and so you have to get another lamb, pigeon, goat and then you have to queue up again and it all costs money, it's very expensive, it takes a lot of time and it keeps these guys in a job. And it's sort of good but it doesn't quite work. They know what it means to forgive sins. And they think also 'who does this guy think he is? Only God can do that.' And they think all of that in a nano-second.

So you've got one group who are incredibly disappointed. You've got another group who are incredibly angry. You've got four friends who are incredibly frustrated because they have expended a lot of energy and now they are thinking 'We've got to get him back up through the roof.' You have got a guy thinking 'That's my roof!' And you've got a paralysed man who everyone is looking at, maybe feeling embarrassed thinking, 'I didn't ask for this.'

This is absolutely brilliant. You couldn't make this stuff up. Jesus has everyone exactly where he wants them. He knows what they are all thinking. Jesus knows what is in our hearts. And he says, in effect, 'I know something you don't know yet.'

The blinding truth is this: what this guy *thinks* he needs in life, what this guy has come for is not what he actually needs. And what Jesus is saying, effectively, is: 'I have just given him what he really needs.'

If the man is confused or even upset, I can relate to that. It's not what he thinks he needs. It just doesn't occur to us that the thing that might be missing is forgiveness.

Think about it. You probably wake up in the morning and think 'I need a coffee', or 'I need to sleep longer'. Probably never on the top of your list of things that you think you need is forgiveness. It's not even high up on the list, in fact you don't often even consider that you've sinned. And so when Jesus says 'Son, your sins are forgiven', well that is pretty offensive stuff.

But my primary need *is* forgiveness. What I need is forgiveness.

The teachers of the law were right. No-one could forgive sin but God. I might say 'I forgive you' but your sins would not be forgiven. And then Jesus says, 'But I want you to know that the Son of Man has authority on earth to forgive sins.' This is huge. Jesus wants his listeners to know not just that he has authority to forgive sin, but that he has authority over the results of sin and the consequences of sin. Don't miss this. The consequence of your sin is death. It is eternal separation from God. Jesus is daring to deal with this.

Now, once again, don't hear what I'm not saying. I'm not implying that the man's inability to walk is the result of his personal sin. But it is the result of sin in this world. Sin that causes separation. And that's what Jesus primarily wants to deal with.

If someone is going to embarrass me and claim they can forgive my sin I want to be absolutely certain they can deal with the consequences of my sin as well, or it will mean nothing. I want to know that he has the authority. Jesus says, 'Get up, take your mat, and go home.' And that is what everyone came for. Now everyone's amazed – they have never seen anything like it.

Our real need, not what we want out of life, but what we really need, is to be right with our heavenly Father. What we really need is to be connected, at our deepest level, with God.

And when you realise that you can't do this. Because of your sin, because of your mess. You get your need for forgiveness, that is why Jesus came. To rip down the barrier of sin between you and a holy God. To tear down the problem. So that you can be eternally connected to the Father.

You are forgiven. You are forgiven of everything. Isn't that incredible news? Sin is the root cause of everything that is messed up. Sin breaks and destroys. And it separates us from God. It separates us from people. So he sent Jesus to offer forgiveness.

Back to Jesus. What this audience didn't know, but we do, is that the same man who said 'Rise up and walk', a number of months later would be nailed to a cross and he would die. And he would die to say to you and to me, 'Son, daughter, your sin is forgiven, your price has been paid.'

You are forgiven.

God trades in forgiveness. He loves to give it. David writes as he experiences the loving forgiveness of God.

'As far as the east is from the west,
so far has he removed our transgressions from us.
As a father has compassion on his children,
so the LORD has compassion on those who fear him;'

Psalm 103:12, 13

He forgives all our sins. His forgiveness is total. His forgiveness is complete. We deserve to be treated as slaves, but we are treated as sons. We do not get what we deserve for our sins. So Jesus is all about forgiveness. He is named for forgiveness: 'you are to give him the name Jesus, because he will save his people from their sins' (Matthew 1:21). He went around offering forgiveness because he recognised it – and demonstrated it – as people's greatest need.

And at the end of his time with them, Jesus commissions the disciples. He breathes on them and they receive the Holy Spirit. Then he tells them, 'If you forgive people, they are forgiven. 'If you do not forgive them, they are not forgiven.' The Godhead's DNA, is grace and forgiveness. You are a son of forgiveness. You are one with forgiveness and you are to be filled with it. It must spill out of you. Forgiveness and grace must define us.

Satan wants to play havoc with our lives. He wants to deny you the beauty and freedom of living in forgiveness. In fact whenever you live with unforgiveness…

… you give territory to him.

MOTHER MUGGER!

I overheard a conversation on a train. (It's amazing how fascinating strangers' conversations are.) I listened in.

Teenage son was attempting to mug his mother for £16,000. He'd had an epiphany. He'd learnt something that demanded action. He had worked out that mum had been paid child allowance all his life. He realised this was because of him and for him. He reasoned that she owed him for every week of his life. He was intent in claiming that which was his. The debate was raging. Teenage son thought he was winning the argument and was obviously banking on settling out of court for a marginally lesser sum. Mum was not going down without a fight. She fired her response on teenage son like a machine gun: 'Well you owe me...' and out it came, for the cooking, the cleaning, the ironing, the taxiing, a fulsome list of estimates for the previous sixteen years. Teenage son looked crestfallen. Meanwhile, Dad continued reading the *Daily Mirror*, oblivious.

The truth is that most of us think that someone, somewhere, owes us. Someone let us down. Someone hurt us. Someone should pay. None of us are immune.

STUCK

Have you ever got your head stuck in the railings? I mean completely stuck. Or your fingers stuck in a coke can? Or perhaps your foot, your shoelace in the escalator? There is nothing quite like the blind panic when a part of your body gets stuck. That split second when you think 'What if I can't get free?'

You can get spiritually stuck too. This has been described in different ways – the slough of despond, spiritual depression, shovelling snow in a blizzard – but whatever you call it, you just feel stuck.

More often than not, it's your unattended baggage that has got you there. More often than not, the experience of generation after generation tells us that the number one issue leading to that feeling of being stuck is unforgiveness.

It is probably true that struggling to forgive, and particularly an unwillingness to forgive others, is the thing that will keep you stuck, perhaps more than anything else. Inability to release forgiveness disables us in our desire to stand, to be who we are called to be. Forgiving others is one of the most important things we have to do, if we truly want to stand, to walk with God, to go deeper.

We can never fully appropriate sonship until we forgive from our hearts. We can never move in power until we forgive and receive forgiveness. Unforgiveness is the root cause of intense bitterness and anger and these so easily colour every part of our lives.

Forgiveness is crucial.

THE ARENA OF GRACE AND THE ARENA OF RIGHTS

One of the most important words in the New Testament is the word 'grace'. We have been saved by grace and it forms God's operational DNA. The word means a free gift for the undeserving. It's the word of the new covenant with God. The old covenant seemed far more transactional. You had to do certain things, behave in certain ways, and you generally got what you deserved. The new covenant is a covenant in Jesus' blood and it is predominantly a covenant of grace. You get what you don't deserve, and you don't get what you do.

This world is the Arena of Rights. It is a place infected by sin. Jesus applies grace in all its glory. He comes down to us. He saves us. And when he does, he offers to remove us from the Arena of Rights, and take us up to the Arena of Grace.

If I'm free of unforgiveness, I'm free to live in grace. But if I start to demand my rights, I have to move out of the Arena of Grace to the Arena of Rights, where there is little mercy, just law and legalism. There the Accuser, for that is what Satan is called, is free to mess with me. I have moved into his arena.

Satan can't get at you while you are under grace. But if he can get you to move away down to the Arena of Rights, if he can manipulate you away from grace, then he has got you.

YOU OWE, YOU PAY

Ask any bank. Ask any payday loans company. They know the deal. When it comes to debt. When it comes to what we owe, there is one simple principle in this life:

YOU OWE – YOU PAY

Peter has someone who has sinned against him, someone who is a debtor (Matthew 18:21). He comes to Jesus attempting to get some wisdom. And in response, Jesus does what he so often does – he tells a story. This one is about a master who wants to settle accounts with his servants (Matthew 18:23–35).

As he begins this settling, a man who owes him ten thousand talents is brought to him. Since he is unable to pay, the master orders that he, his wife and his children, along with all that he has, is sold to repay the debt. One talent in Jesus' day was a stack of cash. In a whole year, all the taxes collected in Judea and Samaria as tribute to Rome added up to only six hundred talents. Ten thousand talents is a whole lot of money. Jesus is saying 'Think of the biggest number you can and double it.' When we were kids we would have said 'a trillion pounds'. I have now discovered, post 'credit crunch', that a trillion is actually a real number, usually with a minus in front of it. This servant owed that much.

So we get an incredibly generous master and we get an incredibly stupid servant, who has blown an amount of cash roughly equivalent to the national debt of a small European country.

This master settles accounts. You owe, you pay. Matthew knows about settling accounts because he's a tax collector. That's what they do. So the time has come and the master says, 'Sell him, his wife, his children, sell all they have.' Which sounds incredibly harsh but in Jesus day this was no surprise. What is surprising is what happens next. The servant falls on his knees before the master. 'Be patient with me', he begs, 'and I will pay back everything.'

And we think: 'No you won't. This is the equivalent of a small European country's national debt, and you don't earn very much, you're a servant, how in the world are you going to pay all this back?'

But the master is moved with compassion. He looks at this frightened fool, and he's moved with pity. He does two things. First, he releases the man, saves his family, frees his children. The servant is released.

But then the master goes way beyond that. He forgives the debt. Now you've got to think about this for a moment. This is a huge amount of money. And it doesn't just disappear. Somebody has to pay. Somebody has to take the loss. But who?

Many of you have hung around in church long enough to know the answer: the Master pays. The king is offering a whole new system of debt management:

YOU OWE – I PAY.

This is the economy of grace, of forgiveness. The kingdom of God is a kingdom of grace. Our king says, 'I will pay the insurmountable debt. I will take the hit. I will suffer the loss. I will take the whole cost on myself so you can go free. You owe, I'll pay.' That's grace.

Pause for a moment. This is our story. This is our story of grace.

Jesus continues and something just mind-blowing happens. You have to read it again to check it is really happening. The servant goes out. He is free. He has just been forgiven a monumental debt and he is free. Then he meets a fellow servant who owes him something, let's say a cinnamon latte by comparison. And you would think he's going to flow with kindness, say something like, 'Friend, latte, shmatte, who cares, have it on me.' But no, he grabs him and seizes him. This isn't even: 'Next time you go and get a coffee, get mine.' Or 'When you get paid I want that hundred denarii back.' No. He seizes him by the throat and starts to choke him. And something dreadful is exposed. This stupid, stupid slave, who has received the most amazing grace, just hasn't entered into the grace economy at all. He's supposed to show some of the same grace, but he chooses instead to operate in rights.

His fellow servants are so disturbed, of course they are. This is unnatural, this is wrong.

What is even more disturbing is that servant is me. That servant is you. Because all of us do this. All of us have this incredible opportunity to live as a child of the living God, and so often we live out of our rights and our opinions. And it just gets you stuck. It makes a mockery out of what Jesus came to do.

Then in anger the master turns him over to the jailers to be tortured until he should pay back all he owed. 'Take him away,' the master says, 'leave him there until he pays back the unpayable debt.' Which is not going to happen. Because the unpayable debt is … unpayable. Who are the torturers? Could it be Satan and his demons? Because you gave him *topos*? Did you give him a permission slip? Did you unintentionally say, tell you what, you can mess with my life? Did you step into and live according to the Arena of Rights?

And then comes one of the most frightening verses in the Bible, 'This is how my heavenly Father will treat each of you, unless you forgive your brother or sister from your heart' (Matthew 18:35). Forgiveness is so important. It's not an option. It's a necessity.

Don't forget, the enemy is described as a thief. He wants to rob you of grace. He wants to hand you over to the torturers. Many of us have at different times chosen rights. We are reaping the whirlwind, and we are stuck.

You know what? I have been forgiven a mountain of debt. If you hurt me, and I choose grace, I forgive you. You owe me nothing. I choose to rip up the IOU. You go free and so do I. This is so important. Whatever has been done to you, hear this:

1. Nobody has harmed us as much as God has forgiven us.
2. Unforgiveness is totally binding. It imprisons people.

We can be so negative. We insist on feeding at the tree of rights – we are full of judgment. It's why we are unhappy, often fault-finding and prone to putting others down.

But if we will forgive … you know what happens? We find freedom. Freedom to go deeper. Freedom to be ourselves. Freedom to pursue the life that God has called us to. Free and empowered to live the kingdom. We become unstuck.

Forgiveness is the key to your freedom. It's essential in your growth. But it's also a lifestyle that we are called to move in.

Let's do this. Let's do this now.

─────────────────── SO: ───────────────────

There is something wonderful about receiving real correspondence, by which I mean, not email, text or tweet, but a letter. How about sending some letters, handwritten on decent paper with a quality pen?

- Letters to say 'thank you'
- Letters to say sorry, to ask forgiveness
- Letters to forgive and free up others

You might also like to read:

Total Forgiveness, R T Kendall (Hodder & Stoughton 2003)

10.

MENDER FOREVER

Above all else, guard your heart, for everything you do flows from it.

Proverbs 4:23

•

'One ought to hold on to one's heart; for if one lets it go, one soon loses control of the head too.'

Friedrich Nietzsche (1844–1900)

Stuff, baggage. We all have it. Experiences, attitudes, defences, wounds, scars, issues, pasts which trip us up, weigh us down, stop us really walking with God, stop us standing up and really being who we are called to be.

At a conference recently an elderly lady came to speak to me. As a minister's wife she had served the church selflessly for over fifty years. Broken, she shared some of her distant past and how she had never really felt valued, or useful, or loved. In so many ways, she was a very godly lady. Yet her beliefs about herself were ungodly. And deeply damaging. Deep down, in her heart, she believed that she was of no value, useless, unloved. She found herself in agreement with Satan about herself. She believed his lies. Her heart was damaged.

We prayed and then we spoke about walking in the opposite spirit. She went away to write down all the things that her heavenly Dad really thought about her – things like: *I am precious and honoured in God's sight. He loves me and values me* (from Isaiah 43:4) *I am greatly loved by my Father and he has made me his child* (from 1 John 3:1). She resolved to commit them to memory by reading them every morning and every evening for six weeks. She agreed to pray them over herself. I don't know the end of the story, but I do know that she is a beautiful, special and gifted lady. She is loved and cherished by her heavenly Dad and I know she needed release from the bondage of ungodly belief.

Or take Andrea. Andrea had a hard childhood. Her mother didn't want her and her father was never around. Neither was very interested in how she did at school, or what she did outside of school. Only that she did not disgrace or embarrass them. Andrea found love and attention in the church, and gave her life to Jesus when she was a young girl. As a teenager she fell in love with the first boy who gave her time and attention. He subsequently dumped her. Andrea loves Jesus, but has massive issues with rejection.

Andrea believes that her heavenly Father is utterly faithful. She sings songs about it. She knows memory verses that proclaim it. But if you probe a little deeper, it's clear that in her heart she doesn't actually believe they are *for her*. What she actually believes is that *she* will be rejected. Everything she says and does is tainted with the lie that she will be rejected.

And somehow she always seems to be the one left out.

Why is that? Well, partly it's that nobody wants to hang out with Miss Pitiful. Honestly, nobody looking round a room at a party thinks, 'I know, I'll go hang around with the kid who looks like she hates herself – she'll be fun!'

Andrea knows this only too well. And somehow, in her heart, she believes that her heavenly Father responds like that as well. Which makes absolute sense to her right now, but to Father God, it is a lie. And so, she finds herself out of agreement with the Godhead. And in agreement with Satan. Her heart is damaged. And she is stuck.

Do Christians really need inner healing? 'No, Karl', you assure me, 'since the moment I accepted Christ as Lord I have not for a moment felt a shred of insecurity or doubt. I have not known the slightest twinge of anger or resentment or jealousy or unforgiveness. I have lived in the fullness of salvation every single day from that day to this.'

Come on. You know that isn't true. We all struggle with identity, with brokenness, with a whole host of things. And yet, a question lingers, prevents us admitting it: 'Wasn't it all dealt with at the Cross? What's wrong with me? Why do I still struggle?'

The truth is, it was dealt with at the cross. But as with sonship and with unity and with power and anointing, we have to *appropriate* that forgiveness and that healing and that salvation. We have to take hold of it, own it, live as if we are healed and saved. As we know we are.

SCARS

All the things that we did are forgiven, but we may still carry scars. The negative things spoken 'over' us may need to be dealt with. If the things done to us or even by us linger, we still believe some of them, and they can cause spiritual damage.

The consequences of an unhealed heart are significant. It can rob us of the life God has for us. It has serious implications for our missional potential – it's hard to love others when we haven't learned to love ourselves. Forgiven people have an opportunity to help other people get forgiven. But if you are not forgiven yourself – if you haven't really *experienced* that forgiveness – how do you communicate that you can be free? Healed people have an opportunity to minister healing to others, but hurt people hurt people, and damaged people damage people.

It also has serious implications for our ministries. An unhealed heart, loaded with unattended issues, can be the root cause of ineffective ministry. Years of failing ministries can often be attributed to unhealed hearts, to 'orphan' spirits. Jesus calls us to go into all the world, preach and teach and make disciples. But if we do that out of duty, it just becomes a task and people just become projects.

So you came to the cross and you were forgiven, but maybe there were some things that needed to be specifically confessed or dealt with and prayed through. There could be a number of things that have damaged your heart and the way you think about yourself and others and God. Maybe somebody said something enough times that you began to believe that about yourself. Perhaps that you are stupid, or a failure, or you'll always be ignored. So you have never fully accepted your true identity in God. Satan has you bound. Maybe you were deprived of love when you were growing up. Your parents didn't do a good job. Maybe they did the best they could with what they had, because what they received wasn't very good either.

Many of us hold ungodly beliefs, issues with approval, addiction, appetite, and many more things. I have issues about my body image. I have issues about what people think about me. It's really, really hard for a guy who has to stand in front of hundreds of people several times a week, when Satan whispers: 'You are fat and they don't even like you!' And you are not even mature enough in your walk with Jesus to not be concerned about that.

Let me show you how this works. We have filters. We apply these filters to everything, to all truth. Which means we see and experience truth differently, often depending upon the experiences we have had of life. So, we might all believe and be able to quote Zephaniah 3:17,

> 'The LORD your God is with you, he is mighty to save. He will take great delight in you, he will quiet you with his love, he will rejoice over you with singing.'

> (NIV 1984)

We might stick that on our fridges, or our make-up mirrors. We might recite it and even claim it for ourselves. And yet, if your heart is damaged, if you have not known love demonstrated by your earthly father, but only abuse, you might actually refuse to accept it. Your experience of fear in childhood may mean that you come with that filter. You might say 'the Lord is with me' and trust it in theory, but you find you are unable to put your full weight behind it. You'll struggle to have faith in it, because you have not dealt with the underlying lie that tells you that you need to be afraid. Or you will be targeted, hurt or unloved.

If we want to be free and we want those around us to know God, then we've got to deal with our ungodly beliefs. We need to get our hearts healed. And the really good news is that God is in the business of healing today, and his healing is available to you.

One of the names that God gives himself, a name that is part of his DNA, is 'Healer'. It's found in Exodus 15:26. He is called *Jehovah Rapha*, usually translated 'the God who heals'. Jehovah can also be translated, 'God forever'. *Rapha* comes from the Hebrew word meaning 'to mend by stitching'. It means to restore, to heal, to make healthy. *Jehovah Rapha*. Mender forever. At the heart of his character, our God, is healing forever. He is the God who mends forever.

The anointing that Jesus embraces and operates out of is a healing anointing. He loves to mend. In his very first public speaking engagement, it is this characteristic that he chooses to emphasise when he announces his ministry.

> '*The Spirit of the Lord is on me,*
> *because he has anointed me*
> *to proclaim good news to the poor.*
> *He has sent me to proclaim*
> *freedom for the prisoners*
> *and recovery of sight for the blind,*
> *to set the oppressed free,*
> *to proclaim the year of the Lord's favour.'*
>
> Luke 4:18, 19; Isaiah 61

Jesus describes himself as the binder of broken hearts. Mender. Healer. The picture that we have is one of a clay pot that has been absolutely shattered. Have you ever felt like that? Your life has just been shattered. David knew this when he cried out in Psalm 51 for a new heart to be created in him. And God, *Jehovah Rapha*, is the supergluing God, who takes all those shards and pieces of your broken pot life and puts it all together.

SOZO

Jesus' commission is for restoration and salvation. Probably the most succinct declaration of Jesus' commission is found in Luke 19:10. Zacchaeus has run ahead and climbed a sycamore tree. And if you know the story from Sunday school Jesus spots him and says 'Zacchaeus come down immediately, I must stay at your house today'. And Jesus does something incredible, he brings some kind of inner healing to Zacchaeus so that Zacchaeus' life is completely transformed, he gives back money to those he has stolen from or cheated, he is a changed man. Jesus declares the kingdom of God, saying 'Today salvation has come to this house, because this man, too, is a son of Abraham. For the Son of Man came to seek and save the lost' (Luke 19:5, 9, 10).

This is vitally important. Because when we understand what Jesus did with Zacchaeus, we understand what he wants to do with us. The word 'save' is a translation of the Greek word *sozo* – which gets translated 'cured, get well, made well, restore and save.' Paul uses *sozo* in a similar sense: 'If you declare with your mouth, 'Jesus is Lord,' and believe in your heart that God raised him from the dead, you will be saved' (Romans 10:9). The word appears again when Jesus heals the sick woman, 'Jesus turned and saw her. "Take heart, daughter," he said, "your faith has healed you." And the woman was healed at that moment' (Matthew 9:22). Again to the blind man '"Go," said Jesus, "your faith has healed you"' (Mark 10:52). *Sozo.* Again Jesus uses it to communicate the restoration of the inner person – when the demon possessed man is delivered, 'Those who had seen it told the people how the demon-possessed man had been cured' (Luke 8:36). *Sozo.*

Sozo is used over a hundred times in the New Testament. Traditionally we have reduced its meaning to 'spiritual salvation' and made it all about being right with God and fit for heaven. It does mean this, but there is more to it than this. Just as Jesus comes to restore all things, there are no aspects of life that are outside of his ability and desire to apply *sozo*. That's why he came. To heal. To restore. To mend. He wants to heal your heart. He wants to bind up and heal broken and damaged hearts.

Why? Because your heart is like a centre. You can cut off a hand or cut out an eye and still be saved (Matthew 5:29, 30). But your heart? Out of the overflow of the heart the mouth speaks (Matthew 12:34). The Lord looks to the heart. We are called to love him with our heart, mind, soul and strength (Matthew 22:37; Deuteronomy 6:5).

And a damaged heart cripples us. The wounds of the heart are agony. We remember only too clearly the times when we have had our hearts broken. We know what rejection feels like; unrequited love; loss. We know the disappointment of trust broken. The pain of loneliness. The weight of living with an unforgiving spirit. Of knowing that we've failed. Again. And again. We know the pain of our own self-loathing. These heart pains cut deep. They are debilitating. What happens to our hearts is so important.

Romans 10:9 claims that what we believe with our hearts is vital for salvation: because, 'if you confess with your mouth, "Jesus is Lord" and believe in your heart that God raised him from the dead, you will be saved'. So what we believe (in our heart) is significant, important, crucial even.

Sports psychologists know this well. That's why they have jobs! The tennis coach who yells out *'Yes* you can' just at the moment when you believe you can't possibly reach that shot, amazingly, turns out right. If on the other hand you are told that you are lacking in comparison to others, or will never succeed, you can easily begin to believe that with your heart. Although very probably it's something more subtle, like unreliable. Untrustworthy. Not quite good enough. Not talented enough. Not important enough. You start to live under that belief. You never quite become all that you could be – the real you. This is particularly difficult when it is instilled in childhood. You learn to erect walls.

Our hearts are our motivators, and we do what we do because of what is inside our hearts. It's what's in you, that ultimately comes out of you. 'Guard your heart above all else, for it determines the course of your life' (Proverbs 4:23, NLT); 'The good person out of the good treasure of his heart produces good, and the evil person out of his evil treasure produces evil, for out of the abundance of the heart his mouth speaks' (Luke 6:45, ESV). And if what is in you is a heart damaged by rejection and fear, then what is going to come out will probably be suspicion and mistrust. However, if you can get the love and grace of God in your heart – if you can be whole-hearted and healed-hearted, then the consequences can be mind-blowing.

Of course Father God knows this. He says 'I will give them a heart to know me' (Jeremiah 24:7).

And again he promises, 'I will give you a new heart and put a new spirit in you; I will remove from you your heart of stone and give you a heart of flesh' (Ezekiel 36:26).

You see. Inner healing. It's not pop psychology. It's an application of the cross of Jesus Christ.

Read John 21. Really read it. Open your Bible and read it.

RE-DO YOU

Take Peter. He is Jesus' best pal. If anyone was supposed to get it right, he was. Peter had been there through all the miracles, listened to all the teaching and was the strong right hand man. But when push came to shove by a fire in a courtyard, Peter caved in. He failed. He denied Jesus. He said, 'I don't know who he is'.

And just as the cock crowed Jesus turned and looked at him. Do you know how much that busted him? Of course you do. Because you know Jesus, it wasn't a look of condemnation. It wasn't a look of 'I'm going to get you!' It was just a look of love. A look of, 'I love you'. And that just broke Peter's heart.

So Jesus comes again. And he does his thing, healing. He says 'I want to mend your heart'. He comes with his incredible miracle working power and says: 'Put your net over the other side, and we'll get some fish'. They haven't caught anything. He knows that. But Jesus needs to remind Peter that he can do anything. He's in the business of fish. And he's in the business of miracle-working mending power.

He comes to you and he wants to remind you that he can do anything. He can superglue your heart in such a way that although you may be able to see the joins, it's mended. Stuff that was said to you and stuff that was done to you. He comes with his gentle friendship. Don't you love that? He says, 'Do you know what – I love you. I want to serve you. Just come and eat.' Jesus comes with gracious restoration.

What was Peter expecting? He might have hoped to be restored by Jesus, one day. But to lead the ministry? He'd think he'd blown it. Completely. Most leaders think something like this: 'If they really knew me, they would never elect me. They would never want me as pastor.' But Jesus healed Peter. Totally healed him. If he hadn't done that, every single time Peter stood up and preached, Satan would have said 'Yeah but you are a failure, you rejected Jesus. Who gave you the right and the authority to preach?'

Jesus says, in effect, 'Let's do business.' He puts his finger exactly where it hurts. 'This is the pain, this is where it started, this is the problem. Do you love me? Do you remember you said you didn't even know me? Will you feed my sheep? Will you feed my lambs? Do you even like me, Peter?' Peter is offended. 'Yes, Lord, you know that I love you.' Then Jesus says, 'Will you be my hands and my feet? Will you be my servant?'

It's an incredible commission. And it all comes out of a gracious God and a healed heart. You want to do community – you need your heart healed? You want to be used for transformation of your city? You need to get your heart healed.

THE EXCHANGE

Father God operates a divine exchange, a swap shop. He wants to do some incredible exchanges. In Isaiah 61, the prophet speaks of a time when God is going to re-do things. He is working on behalf of the poor, the broken, the bound, the sick, and the disabled. They are going to become 'oaks of righteousness, a planting of the Lord for the display of the his splendour.' In other words – this exchange is going to show God's glory and prove his righteousness.

He gives beauty and he takes away ashes

In biblical times, it was customary for people to sit in a pile of ashes when in deep mourning. Where the focus has been the stuff that is lost, where the context is death, he is going to exchange it for the reality that is life and beauty, and not least your beauty (v 3). He is going to remind you of how beautiful he is, how beautiful his creation is and how beautiful you are! In those days oil had a variety of uses, from anointing kings and prophets to lighting homes and cooking food. Here the reference is to oil applied to the face. Oil to make you shine. He'll lavish such joy on you. Joy for life and joy for him. You will praise and you will display his glory, his life, his restoration. It's time to shine.

He gives relief and praise and takes away despair

The spirit of heaviness, hopelessness, broken hearts, inner hurts. They steal joy. God's exchange is the ability to praise and worship him. God does not promise that there will be no pain and no sorrow and no disappointment. This side of heaven there will be all these things. But the exchange that he does promise is that these things will not bring despair. We are not hopeless (vv 1–3).

So many of us are destructively burdened. We are carrying things that are not ours to carry. Even that which *is* ours to carry is really heavy. We forget that his burden is light. We have not tapped into the truth that if we ask him, he wants to carry for us. He wants to carry with us. It is as we worship; it is as we face the Father, that our heavy spirits are raised up and exchanged for praise (v 3).

We will know and see his beauty. We will know his joy and shine – even when life sucks! God is going to rebuild ancient ruins. He's going to restore places long devastated. He will renew ruined cities. He will rebuild our lives and make them God-centred. He will mend our broken hearts (vv 4–7).

He will exchange our ruined ambition and shattered dreams for his hope

They will be God-crafted and eternal. Where there are shattered dreams and ambitions, where families are ruined and relationships shattered. Where we have had hope and life stolen from us – he is going to exchange our despair for his joy.

God's going to re-do, and he wants to do it now.

——————— SO: ———————

God's got a book out. It's rammed full of truth, wisdom and direction for your life. If you let the word of God fill your heart it will change your life. Generations of Jesus followers have understood the need to 'hide the word of God in your heart' (see Psalm 119:11).

I have three challenges for you:

- Write out ten Bible verses about your identity and power as a child of God. Read them each morning and each evening. Place the card in your wallet, on your car dashboard. Get the Word of God into your heart!
- There is significant evidence that your mind receives things subliminally. Record your voice on your phone reading the truth of God's Word for you and play it as you sleep.
- Start to pray the Word of God, 'Father you have said … Jesus you have promised … Holy Spirit I invite you to … as your Word says.'

PART 4.

STAND OUT
STAND BY

•

I looked for someone among them who would build up the wall and stand before me in the gap on behalf of the land so I would not have to destroy it, but I found no one.

Ezekiel 22:30

IT'S STRANGE REALLY, IN A CULTURE WHICH WORSHIPS THE INDIVIDUAL, HOW MUCH GENERIC YOU COME ACROSS. EVERYONE SEEMS TO WANT TO BE DIFFERENT LIKE EVERYBODY ELSE. AS YOU STAND UP AND STAND FIRM, YOU WILL BEGIN TO STAND OUT. NOT JUST FOLLOWERS, BUT LEADERS, NOT JUST SAME OLD SAME OLD, BUT STAND OUT MODELS. SO STAND OUT FOR JESUS. STAND OUT WITH JESUS. STAND OUT IN JESUS. AND STAND OUT TOGETHER.

11.

TWO BALL SCREWBALL

I sought to hear the voice of God and climbed the topmost steeple,
but God declared: 'Go down again – I dwell among the people.'
John Henry Newman (1801–1890)

I was driving back up to Scotland from England on the M6 motorway, passing the hilly Cumbrian village of Shap. The blizzard was making the journey difficult. Visibility was minimal. It took every ounce of effort to keep focused on the job in hand: driving safely home.

And there it was. An ice cream van. In the inside lane. Just at that moment, God planted a thought in my mind. In that second something became so clear to me that I couldn't ignore it. God showed me just what the church has been doing for decades. The right thing. At the wrong time. In the wrong place. In the wrong way.

We have positioned ourselves wrongly and our message seems irrelevant. It's killing the church. It's killing our message. There is no doubt that in our best moments, and with our best intentions, we have tried to be outward facing. We have certainly been conscious of being 'on mission', and yet, it is just not working, and it's killing us. There is a pretty long list of failings – of fundamental mission-mistakes – that we have all been party to.

There is our love of talking much and strategising lots, and yet doing precious little. We entertain a quaint belief that everyone out there is just yearning to come to us – if only we can create just the right event to invite them to. We obsess over the latest evangelism strategies, rolling out of the biggest, shiniest mega-churches. 'This'll make them come', we enthuse. And too often, we are disappointed.

As far as mission is concerned, we've done it all. We have exploded, been friendly, explored and marched. Our churches have been cafes and become messy and we've done an awful lot of courses. While we haven't found the golden bullet (maybe there isn't one), some of it has been successful. But most of it hasn't made a significant difference. The church collectively seems to have been in decline for quite a while.

We need to reposition.

See, until we address this, we will continue to offer ice-creams and two ball screwballs at forty miles an hour, in a January snow blizzard, near Shap, in the wilds of nowhere, to no-one. It's as random as that. We convince ourselves we're heading in the right direction, and convince ourselves and others that we feel good about doing so. But I think, in truth, we gave up.

Our world lives under a misconception about the God who loves us. We need to put that right. The predominant position of the church must not be battening down hatches and hiding away. We've spent too many years clinging on to our 'get out of hell free' cards. We need to reposition and reposition now. We need to boldly take hold of our calling. We need to walk confidently in our anointing. We need to be the church of Jesus Christ in this place, and to this generation. To achieve that, we need to be open to change and to a more creative approach to mission.

And we are. There's a stirring in the culture of the church and the Spirit is moving us forward. We're starting to get it. The church is repositioning. It may not be comfortable. The position we need to take is one sculpted by the love, power and creativity of God. God for us and God in us.

The church's position has to be missional. We need to be *missional*.

GO AND DWELL

By 'missional' we mean more than just doing mission. It doesn't mean arranging events and firing them at people, or towards people. Adopting a missional posture is not an isolated event, although it may include events. Missional is not the result of a programme, or a course.

A missional position is not so much 'come and see', it's not about developing an attracting strategy. Missional is much less hit and run than that. It is definitely not Christian guerrilla warfare!

Missional is more about 'Go and dwell'. Think about it, we are called to be Jesus people. We become the hands, feet and mouth of Jesus. We are the body of Christ – and this metaphor is deliberate and uncompromising. Jesus is the incarnate one – the one who moved into the neighbourhood, wore the skin and lived amongst us, he fleshed out God for us. As one of us. Fully God, fully man.

The trouble is, many Christians embrace the idea, and love the concept, and stop there. But missional cannot be, or rather cannot stay, theoretical. Missional is by definition an outward facing expression of the God life. It's practical. It's a living orientation towards being – modelling, speaking, showing – Jesus. Being Jesus before people and indeed for people. The fact is people are the priority. We need to do more than deliver the message, we need to be the message. Preaching the message, coupled with being the message. This has never been more important! The fact is, for many we come into contact with, we are the best, and sometimes the only, Jesus they are going to see.

Missional is being, as much as it is doing. It acts, of course it acts, but it is. It exists. To live from a missional, outward facing position requires careful consideration. There needs to be vision. There needs to be strategy. Plans and provisions certainly need to be made. But before all that, it needs commitment – it needs you!

It needs you to stand up and then out. To resolve to be the real you. The true you. It needs you to determine to become more like him. It needs you to be the best you you can become. You do it for him. You do it for you. You do it for the world.

This is exciting. Father God wants to take you and I on a journey. It's an incredible journey that will bring us closer to him, both for his delight and for the sake of everyone else around us.

MISSIONAL COMMUNITIES

The Holy Spirit has led our church into a new form of missional awareness and activity. We agreed as a leadership that we needed to get out more, face outwards more, and filter all we did through the needs of those who currently didn't belong to us. We set up new groups we call Missional Communities. That just about describes them. Communities or families on mission.

TWO BALL SCREWBALL|153

Not one Missional Community was suggested, or set up, by me. We just asked people to pray and, inspired by the Holy Spirit, to go with the dreams that God placed in their hearts. We as a leadership have had to let go, to see what God will do. To trust him. And not to control things.

And the Missional Communities formed. It is beautiful to see, it is the church going out to the people. Why did we ever focus so much on trying to get people to the church? New groups are springing up all the time as people open up to the Spirit and allow him to guide and inspire them. They are all very different, all very creative. It is all a little messy!

Happy Hens

We have one Missional Community which ministers to excluded, marginalised teenagers. We call it Happy Hens. This group is based on a 500-acre farm, which has been released by a couple in our congregation for just this purpose. 12,000 hens – many more thousand eggs – and kids who have some learning struggles, and some behavioural challenges. The kids are learning people skills. They are loved and nurtured and helped to find their way in life. And as they are loved, they see Jesus.

Square Wholes

We have another Missional Community which ministers to adults with learning difficulties. It is built around that Scottish cultural icon, the ceilidh, a sort of barn dance on steroids. As people dance and sing together, as they listen to stories and eat together, they show love and see demonstrated the incredible grace of Father God.

STEP

STEP sees the local high school as its community, prays for it, runs parenting classes, feeds teachers at parents' evenings and paints the school building. They are making the name of Jesus famous in the school.

Strong Tower

Strong Tower ministers the love of God to a less affluent estate in the city. They meet in the pub on the estate and go on the streets, they mentor kids who are struggling academically and emotionally, getting to know the teenagers and building relationships, being Christ for those who need Jesus.

Centurian

This group ministers to soldiers – men who see active service in places like Afghanistan. It supports their families, and keeps them closely in contact with the Church. It grew out of one family's Spirit-given passion for ministry among the armed forces.

Streetlife

Streetlife reaches out to girls in the sex industry both on the streets and in the lap dancing bars in Edinburgh. It's messy, at times disturbing, and it raises some great and complex moral ethical and relational questions – and so, it should. But Jesus is walking the streets and in the bars and I think he smiles.

These are just some of our Missional Communities. The Spirit has inspired, and is releasing many, many others. That's missional church. These are not chance happenings. They are God inspired. These are the places the Jesus takes us when we let him lead us.

———————————— SO: ————————————

The vast, vast majority of people that you meet, who live around you, have no realistic concept of God and no relationship with Jesus. You do! Could it be that there is a specific correlation between those two facts? How you live and what you say make a massive difference. Ask yourself two questions:

- Who has God intentionally placed around your life?
- What is your story? Write it down. Now read it again, and listen to it as if you had never been in a church in your life, never heard of Jesus. Now remove all the words you wouldn't understand, all the Christian jargon.
- Look for opportunities as you live the story to share the story of your life.

Read on …

12.

BABEL REVISITED

One of the marvellous things about community is that it enables us to welcome and help people in a way we couldn't as individuals. When we pool our strength and share the work and responsibility, we can welcome many people, even those in deep distress, and perhaps help them find self-confidence and inner healing.
Community and Growth, Jean Vanier (2006)

•

One can acquire everything in solitude except character.
Five Short Novels of Stendhal, Stendhal (1958)

The Bible stories of Babel and Pentecost are fascinating mirror accounts. Babel is the Old Testament account of a people building a tower, seeking to make a name for themselves, wanting to be God. God confuses them by giving them different languages and they separate. Pentecost is the New Testament account of a people waiting for God. Seeking to make a name for Jesus. God empowers them with speaking in other tongues but by being heard in their own languages, they unify and then change the world. There is something about unity, something about community that is powerful, incredibly powerful.

We are family. We are called to be family. It's that simple.

Transformation is a team thing. It doesn't take away from our uniqueness. It enhances it. Each of us is special. Each of us is carefully crafted by the Father's hand. Each of us is to experience extraordinary transformation, and it'll be as a sign and a catalyst for the transformation of all around us. But, we're not meant to experience it in isolation. The sense of 'we' is crucial. Together, we carry community.

Contemporary Western Society loves the individual. The mantra of our society is 'Look after number one'. There's little encouragement to do 'we'. Even in church we have emphasised individual spiritual disciplines over corporate ones: 'Read your Bible. Pray every day. Do this and you'll grow, grow, grow!' We sing about, 'This little light of mine' and 'You in your small corner and I in mine'. The onus is on the individual.

Ancient Hebraic society was different. God had set them up to understand and embrace the truth that community enabled them to stand as the people of God. They had just forgotten it. Amongst many other things, Pentecost re-awakened the community consciousness in the people of God. The early church didn't just need power, they needed together power. They knew they needed to be together to grow, to know God, and to survive. They got the notion of 'we'. The Apostle Paul argues this in his letter to the church in Ephesus. He says even though we have the life of the Trinity in us we will continue to live in immaturity and experience lack until we learn how to walk in unity with one another.

We have one Spirit, he says. One Lord. One God (Ephesians 4:4–6). But unless we have real unity in the faith we will act like babies, blown around and deceived and unable to stand. You and I need others. It's not simply desirable, it's essential. Why? Because God created you and I to need others. This need is built in. You and I are incomplete without a team.

And this is all modelled for us by Father God. After all he is team. He is in community. You and I are created in his image. We cannot fully reflect the 'imago Dei', or live out the 'Mission Dei' alone in our little corners, with our little candles.

BETTER TOGETHER!

At Central, we teach every young disciple of the necessity of three kinds of relationships. Three key people you need to have in your life.

Firstly, you need to have someone who you can:

Sit at the feet of ...

This must be a real person. A real flesh and blood person – not a virtual person. This is not someone whose blog you follow, or whose podcast you subscribe to. Not even someone you can email with your stuff. This is someone who you *know* and just as importantly, someone who knows you. This person needs to be someone who has walked longer and further than you. Someone who has some knowledge of the road ahead and a deep relationship with the Guide of all of our Souls. It has taken me years to get this sorted, but I think I have found, in recent years, a man of God to be this person for me. And I am better for him.

Mike Breen of 3DM teaches a model to clarify the importance of this. His argument says that most disciples want new information from books, preachers or conferences. What they seem to do with that information is to rush to innovate from it. Often that innovation is half-baked, not well-thought through and doomed to failure. Why? Breen argues it's because we are hard-wired to walk in community and learn by imitation. Only then can we move on to innovation. That's the nature of discipleship.

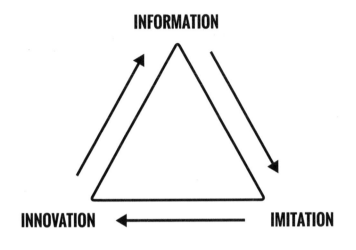

INFORMATION

INNOVATION   **IMITATION**

Secondly, you need someone to:

Look in the eye of ...

We each need a couple of friends who know us intimately. People who are committed to encouraging us to realise all the potential that Father God has placed in us. They'll ask the questions we all need to answer, even when we don't want to answer them – actually, especially when we don't want to answer them! 'What are you learning about Father God and yourself?' 'How are you growing in who God has made you to be?'

Niki and I moved from our last church feeling pretty battered and bruised by what institutional church can do to its leaders. We were aware of the fact that we needed mighty men and women to aid and to support us. Men and women to push us and stretch us, and now and again to chide and embrace us.

Check out the skills of David's warrior pals – look at 2 Samuel 23:8 and 1 Chronicles 18:14–17. The Lord in his love and wisdom has given us such men and women. The benefit is that we can stand together.

The relative growth and health of Central has much to do with the mighty men and the fearless women who invest in the lives of others. To them, I will always be grateful. These close allies are so much in relationship with us, that they can tell us very clearly and simply when we are acting like dopes.

My guys ask me great questions. They drill into my prayer life. My times with the Father. They ask about date nights and parenting. They probe into my use of money. They ask about my physical, emotional and spiritual fitness. They throw questions that provoke the kingdom in me! I know that whatever I do, they will be my cheer section! I know, that because of them, I can be more intimate with my Father, God. I can do that because he, in his wisdom, uses them to help me draw nearer to him.

Thirdly, you need someone who you can:

Pour yourself into . . .

The relationship equation is not complete until there is some output for the support, wisdom and nurturing that you are receiving. Without someone who sits at your feet, you are very likely to become spiritually obese.

All of our leaders and all of our apprentices must have someone that they are apprenticing – someone that they are pouring themselves into. Without it, the other two relationships eventually become unhelpful – because ultimately what comes out, what is passed on, is the aim of anything that is put in.

The quality of community that we must carry is of a different strata than any communities that our world knows of. Indeed part of the problem we face is that we have attempted to replicate the model, style and governance of the communities that we live amongst. We have chaired meetings as if they were the Conservative Club, discussed things as if it was the Golf Club and mistaken theocracy for democracy. There's so much more.

There is a quality of community in the kingdom of God that would take a library of books to try to unpack in any decent way.

If we are going to do community well, there are fundamental truths we need to get. At the heart of true community, and for us to build it well, we need to understand that:

WE IS MORE IMPORTANT THAN ME …

We started with the premise that it is all about you. Now is the point when it's going to sound even more contradicatory.

It's *not* all about you.

It's all about him and therefore all about us. If we see community before we see individuality, then we can handle and truly appreciate diversity in gifts and passions. If 1 Corinthians 12 is to be believed and all gifts are for the common good, then when I preach – we preach. When you sing – we sing. When you account – we account. When he prophesies – we prophesy. Your gifts are my gifts. Your blessing is my blessing. Your pain is my pain.

Now that builds community, because I am grace-bound to meet your need. I am grace-bound to share with you and help lift your burden. And you are grace-bound to help me – because in him we are one, you are me and I am you.

Go …

If you ask most Jesus followers when it was that they grew most in their faith, they will point either to a mission trip they took part in, a youth group they were part of, a CU at university, or to a church planting experience. Missional living provides the most wonderful context for life discipleship.

Indeed missional living is the best context for community, *per se*. When we practice it, reliance on Father God is likely to increase, because this is challenging stuff. Reading of the Word of God increases, because we need to be able to give an answer to the faith we profess. Reliance on each other grows, because we need each other for support, prayer, gifts etc. Prayer life goes through the roof! 'Holy Spirit if you don't show up, we are right royally stuffed! Come Holy Spirit.'

Modelling Jesus' lifestyle becomes more important because you are suddenly the shop window to the Jesus' life. If you are offering transformation, you'd better be showing transformation.

In fact the reality is, you cannot do community without 'Go!'

Living in the hope of a story we write together

Missional vision is vital for radical community. Without it the people perish. There is a strength to any community that can together live in the same rhythm, looking in the same direction. There is power in a community that can believe for something beyond their own needs and can live for a brighter future. And there is no unity like that of a community which lives with the hope of the story they write together. Leaders – give people a vision to live for. Something that is worth dying for. Give them this and you will find that people will follow and flourish and then go on to lead themselves. Where this is practised, community will be built.

TRUTHED IN LOVE

Pastoral care is not just about being nice to people. It's not about soothing and cosseting them. True pastoral care is more about how I help you become more like the person Jesus is moulding you to be. It's how I stand with you in the storms of this life and help you to stand so that you, in turn, might stand with others.

Recently, I heard someone say that most people who left the church claim that the reason they left was because 'they were not looked after'. He asserted that the unwritten contract that the body should make with an individual is 'we will disciple you', not 'we will look after you'. The former is about transformation and the latter about preservation.

I have discovered that many of the pastoral issues I deal with in church life come from those who have known Jesus for many years. They have been Jesus followers for years, yet the community has not discipled them. They have not been truthed in love. No one has said, 'You can't continue to act out of that spirit of insecurity.' No one has corrected a critical spirit. No one challenged spiritual tantrums. No one refused to allow power games to be played in leadership. Consequently people did not grow up in the Lord, and the community continued to be a nursery.

Belonging is more important than behaviour

For years the institution of church has formally and informally excluded people on the grounds of lifestyle and behaviour. Class, colour, gender, and sexual orientation have all been used a barriers to community.

Yet for radical kingdom community to exist, these things are all secondary. It is true that Father God loves you just the way you are. It is also true that he loves you too much to leave you that way. It is further true, that we believe in the power of this kind of community, and we trust in the goal of the Father, Son and Spirit for transformation. If so, we must believe that it is better that all people be part of us, rather than be excluded.

I suggest that a centred theology and a centred ecclesiology, 'we follow Jesus', is far more conducive to kingdom community than a protectionist bounded set, 'you must practice this/behave in this manner, if you are to be part of us!' To exclude people in the way I am talking about is a counterproductive practice. If what we want to achieve is belief and behaviour, it will never happen until there is first a sense of belonging. I also concede that this kind of messy kingdom community is much harder to conceive of and even harder to pastor. It requires more work, and more difficult pastoral conversations. It requires a deeper worked-through teaching ministry, and yet it is more redemptive, more transformatory, more counter-cultural and more Gospel-centred!

Criticism is not always opposition

Criticism can be opposition. It can be negative and it can sap motivation.

But not always. Community is built when we give the benefit of the doubt to one another and assume the best. Now this is tough for those of us with a highly evolved sense of discernment. But nevertheless two things I have found to be true.

Firstly, all criticism is positive. It's true in that there is always something in the criticism that we can learn from. In fact some of the most painful critiques hurt because there is truth at the root of them. Wise community builders will learn to stand long in the glare of unfair and unrighteous criticism. They'll do it so that they and others might grow.

Secondly, opinion is different from counsel. There is a difference between a culture of counsel and a culture of opinion. The difference is in the heart from which it comes. If your heart thinks the best, wants the best and speaks the best, then it is well placed to be wise counsel, counsel that we all need. If, however, it is offered from the heart that doesn't prefer the best – one that thinks and speaks the worst, it is most likely to be a critical spirit and deeply destructive. It busts community wide open!

Lack of unity is devastating within core leadership teams. Do not countenance it for one moment. A city divided against itself will fall. Let me explain why this is the case. I have experienced enough leadership teams that are pulling in different directions to know the colossal pain of this. Your leaders do not need *yes* men and women. But they do need people who are 100% committed to the leader and 100% devoted to the vision. Then, and only then, can real and robust conversations, without suspicion and defensive positioning, become possible. These conversations are life-blood for authentic community.

Leaving is not failure – neither is staying success

Arriving and leaving are a fundamental part of community life. In no way is this statement a green light for people to play church shopping or church hopping! However, there are many who feel that if people leave a church, the leadership must be doing something wrong. There are others who feel that if they don't fit in with a church culture, or don't believe in the leadership, or the vision, they just have to suck it up and passively endure or actively oppose.

People left Jesus' company. People left Paul. Paul and Barnabas split. It would be arrogant to believe that people will never leave us, or that we would never have to leave ourselves. There are times when it's right to leave. When you do – do it well! You never know, you may one day return.

Find a place where you can support the vision 100%, support the leaders and serve Jesus by being in community. Find it and be there.

WATCH YOUR MOUTH!

Proverbs 10:11. 'The mouth of the righteous is a fountain of life.' The Bible says your mouth is a central issue as far as your spirituality is concerned, and as far as community is concerned. It's massively important. This seems strange. Go to any good bookshop, and head to the self-help/improvement section – the one that has all the books on lifestyle and leadership. I guarantee you will not find many, if any, entitled, *Mouth Management to Make you a Better Leader*, or anything of that ilk!

That said, I firmly believe that taking control of the mouth is a means of truly improving as a person. You would be better in any walk of life! You'll lead well, build community better and simply be an all round better person. Most importantly, controlling your tongue will help you to glorify God more effectively. The tongue is your interface with life. We use it to communicate and connect with other people.

It's ultimately the only way that you will know what's going on inside of me. We build people up with it and we cut people down by it.

There is incredible power for good in your tongue. Those of us who have kids know that one word of affirmation, or encouragement, can change anything for them. Our words can empower and energise. Perhaps it can also be said that one careless word can ruin a person.

The quality of community that you carry with you, is determined significantly by what comes out of your mouth.

Speak the truth. Because:

- Lying breaks the heart of God. It flies in the face of who he is. God in his fundamental character is a truth-teller and you cannot underestimate the dissonance that goes on in the heart of a Holy God when we lie.
- Lying destroys trust with everyone in our lives.
- Lying corrodes the inner core of who we are. It is ultimately collusion in the enemy's enterprises.

Speak life. Speak well of people, they are created in the image of God

- You have never met, nor will you ever meet, anyone who Father God does not love.
- You have never met, nor will you ever meet, anyone who Jesus did not die for.
- You have never met, nor will you ever meet, anyone who the Holy Spirit is not pursuing.

Speak well of the Bride of Christ. Jesus is seriously not impressed with his children slagging off his bride. Speak encouragement!

- Tell people you think they are great! It breathes courage into them. I am almost ashamed to admit how much a word of encouragement changes things for me. Tell people you love them! It breathes life into them.

- I LOVE YOU. These words are vital. We all know people who have had their souls seriously damaged because they never heard those three words. Tell those whom you love that you love them. Do it all the time!

AUTHENTIC COMMUNITY

How would others describe you? Are you an open person? Do you tend to keep your cards close to your chest? What about your home? Open, or closed? What about your table? How about your wallet? Your kids?

These may sound like silly questions, but they are not. We cannot build community without openness, and this posture, this attitude, extends into all these areas. To have community we must have things in common, stuff in common, life in common. The New Testament church had a word for this. They called it *koinonia*. We have reduced its meaning by labelling it 'fellowship'. It sounds like quiche and cocktail sausages. But really it's the most authentic form of redemptive community ever seen.

We need to be open in all these aspects of our lives if we are to build authentic community.

It's about open home

Our home is an open home. We always seem to have someone living with us and usually someone else staying. Recently we had a family of four, a mum and three kids, stay in our house for a fortnight. They had nowhere to go. When things in our house were getting overcrowded and at times fraught, another family in church had them stay with them for a further three weeks. During that time we were working on securing a suitable long term living arrangement for them. But until this was possible, we were glad to have them with us. That's *koinonia*. And it's not just about home ownership. It's about car ownership, and even lawnmower ownership (why does *every* household need one of those!).

It's about open family

If my house is not mine and my money is not mine (nor any of my possessions for that matter), then it must follow that my kids are not my possessions either!

In fact at dedication services we talk about the child being on 'loan' from Father God.

This most precious gift of God does not belong to Mum and Dad, they have the child 'on loan'. So, we need, with wisdom and generosity, to share our kids, particularly with those who don't have children. Some would love to have kids, and many just want to be included in family.

Our church, and I am sure the church in general, is not set up to be most helpful and welcoming to single people and that is a crying shame. It is a shame because this kind of authentic community is best set to be extended family for all kinds of people, with all kinds of different life circumstances.

It's about open table

If you want to build community, open your table and eat together. The stories of Jesus very often have, as their context, a table and food: the first miracle of water into wine; the Last Supper; the Wedding Feast of the Lamb. Food is crucial to community.

We read in Acts 2 that, 'they broke bread in their homes and ate together with glad and sincere hearts'. I am sure that they didn't just 'do' communion. With silver chalices or metal shot glasses, hunks of bread or weird wafers. I am convinced that they ate together, proper food. I am also convinced that this was not insignificant in building life-transforming missional community.

There is something about eating together.

Maybe it's transparency. If you want to see the way I parent my kids, the patience I have, or don't have, then come to dinner.

There are no airs and graces at the Martin table. It can be bedlam and it's almost always fun, but it is also raw. And, after you leave and when you reflect, you can be in no doubt that ours is a real family and the Pastor is as fallible as anyone else!

Maybe it's time. I recently read a great book, *The End of Religion*, that says that God moves at three miles an hour. If three miles an hour is the speed that we walk, then that's the speed of love because God comes alongside us. I love that concept. I think it applies here too. Almost everything we do, we do fast – often too fast to spot what God is doing and get with his rhythm and purpose. Sitting down to eat – to break bread – forces us to slow down and even to reflect. It helps us to remember to ask the Holy Spirit, 'What are you doing in this moment? How can I cooperate?' Relational miracles happen around the table.

Every year, Niki and I run a twelve-week intensive discipleship group for emerging leaders. It's pretty full on. The participants commit to reading large chunks of the Scripture together. They commit to practicing spiritual disciplines, to memorising parts of the Word, to learning how to 'pray and minister' and to 'speculating on the power of the Holy Spirit', through a series of weekly challenges. The one thing that makes the group work, however, is that each week on Wednesday the group fasts and then we break the fast at 9pm with a huge meal around our table. I am convinced that it is this simple act that models and builds community. Food is important!

Community is so crucial. If you don't carry it, I'm afraid you don't carry the image of God as you can and are called to do. And in addition to that, a large piece of you – the you that is being transformed and becoming transformation, is missing. It's disabled. We are not complete without community!

The writer to the Hebrews puts it brilliantly:

> … *let us draw near to God with a sincere heart in full assurance of faith, having our hearts sprinkled to cleanse us from a guilty conscience and having our bodies washed with pure water. Let us hold unswervingly to the hope we profess, for he who promised is faithful. And let us consider how we may spur one another on*

towards love and good deeds. Let us not give up meeting together,
as some are in the habit of doing, but let us encourage one another
– and all the more as you see the Day approaching.

Hebrews 10:22–25 (NIV 1984)

KINGDOM COMMUNITY

Show me people who are pursuing Father God and you show me people who are being transformed. People who are holding onto hope without swerving! Show me those people and I will show you people who are meaningfully connected to God and others. People who love and carry kingdom community. People who have learned to stand together.

––––––––––––––––––––––––– SO: –––––––––––––––––––––––––

Have you ever fasted? From food? Probably you have. The challenge here is to fast from negativity. Take a week and determine to only speak positively, if you can manage it, only think positively. Unless you are incredibly holy, you will find this incredibly hard, but it might just change your heart and it will bless your community.

You might also like to read:

The End of Religion, Bruxy Cavey (Navpress 2007)
A Meal with Jesus, Tim Chester (IVP 2011)

13.

DOING IT IS DOING IT

'Freedom lies in being bold.'
Robert Frost (1874–1963)

•

Be on your guard; stand firm in the faith; be courageous; be strong.
1 Corinthians 16:13

Our daughter Abigail had diving lessons at the Commonwealth Pool in Edinburgh for a while, and I was the nominated taxi service. I have to say watching diving lessons is not exactly a thrill a minute.

In fact, the only thing that kept me from extra sermon prep was the appearance of 'Diving Girl' each week. I don't know her name, but she was about twelve years old and she seemed to be one of the better divers at the pool. She had her own coach and each week she treated us to her own little cameo performance. She would confidently climb the steps, all the way up to the ten-metre board. She walked to the edge and looked over. She would place her arms in the traditional diving position. Next, she would look at her coach (who always gave a big grin and a thumbs up). She was a study of concentration. She prepared to dive. She stood and looked again, measuring and estimating angles. Then, the pose would collapse. She'd fling herself back to the stair railing, clinging to it for dear life. Diving girl went through the same routine three times each week, always climbing down for her finale. It became such a regular slot in our Friday diving schedule that, by week four, all the parents were looking up and giving her the thumbs up. Diving Girl's dive had become a focus of community importance! But sadly, Diving Girl never actually took that dive. She clearly had the ability and she would have loved the achievement. Mum, Dad and Coach would have been blessed. We weekly spectators would have been ecstatic! But she never did.

The Holy Spirit is calling us into a dive. A plunge. We are called to immerse ourselves in him and in what he is doing in this world. He is calling us to stand out. Like diving, all it takes is one step. Much of the rest is momentum.

That one step requires balls. It requires real courage. Sons carry courage and Father God is drawn to it. He loves courage.

Hebrews 11 is God's tribute to courage. It's for men and women who took a step – often over the line. They did it not because it was expedient, but rather because it was right. They did it not because it always made sense, but because God asked.

Noah built a boat in the desert. Abraham left to go to the place he was yet to be shown, because God told him to. Moses chose disgrace over position.

There are two phrases in that chapter that resonate deeply: 'God is not ashamed to be called their God' and 'the world was not worthy of them' (Hebrews 11:16, 38).

TWO SWORDS AND A HILL

Let me take you to a moment in Israel's back catalogue. 1 Samuel 14. Context: The Philistines, Israel's arch-enemies, have invaded the land and are holding the nation in bondage. They control all the power and all the blacksmiths. Blacksmiths? Blacksmiths. So any equipment that needed sharpening – ploughshares, axes, swords, for instance – had to be sharpened *by the enemy* (1 Samuel 13:19–22).

Israel has only two swords. Saul's and Jonathan's.

It is what father and son do with their swords that interests us. Saul takes himself and his sword and sits under a pomegranate tree with his leaders. Presumably they talk about how desperate things are, how good things once were and what might be done about the situation.

Jonathan, with the other sword, makes a stand, he takes to a hill. He defeats the enemy and restores the nation. Read the story – Jonathan speculates on the power of God and finds that God is able. He probably assumes that it will be easier to ask forgiveness after the event, than to get permission before it. So Jonathan acts.

Ours is a time for the church to exchange trees for hills. It's time to take a stand. Time for the church to stop huddling around ecclesiastical pomegranate trees, and moaning about our lack of swords and talking about what the church could look like, if we ever took to a hill.

GET OUT MORE

It's time to speculate, to stand upon the power and grace of God. It's time to get out of our buildings, embrace the kingdom of God and become like Jesus. It's time to get active. Time to put one step in front of another. It's time to restore a nation.

There is a time to sit under a tree and anxiously plan, but not very often, and it is not now. The battle is being lost and the name of God is being dishonoured. What is needed is a generation of Jonathans. A generation of armour bearers. A generation of men and women who will not wait for permission to do what is already the will of the Father.

- They will speculate on the power of God.
- They will sense the purpose of God for them and will act on it.
- They will plant churches, initiate kingdom ventures and restore kingdom living.
- They will love on people – how they will love!
- They will take a lead in their communities for the common good and for the glory of God.
- They will know the fact that our best days are before us, not behind us!

Some will say: is it not dangerous to act without permission? Yes, it might be, but you already have all the permission in the world. All the commission of your heavenly father. Go, make disciples, Go, bear my image, participate in my mission. Go love people. A better question might well be what are we waiting for? I have become increasingly aware in my life – both personal and ministry – that inhibition is more limiting, more suffocating, even than prohibition. I tell myself that they won't let me, or like it, but in truth I am just fearful.

As I write, the Western world is experiencing a far reaching crisis of confidence in government, banking, the church and family. We have lost a sense of leadership with integrity and consequently have a skewed perspective on following. Ironically, we know we need leadership, but don't really want to be led. We know we need to lead, but don't want to take risks. We understand that it is great to be decisive, but don't want to make decisions.

We need help!

It would be more than fair to say we are presented with an opportunity to model leadership of a different kind. Indeed, those of us who follow Jesus are compelled to do so. Jesus' followers have an opportunity to redefine healthy, releasing and empowering leadership.

DREAMS TO SCREAMS

There has been a tendency in the contemporary church to idolise *strong leadership*. This has sometimes warped, and morphed into *strong control*. Senior leaders and pastors have had to have their hands on everything. They've insisted on attending all meetings and on having all decisions passed through them.

Such an approach monopolises vision. It shrinks potential. It chokes creativity and frustrates emerging leaders.

I have had nothing directly to do with the most innovative and redemptive enterprises in our church family. All I have done is to provide space and inspiration. *Elephant Juice* is a soup company. A really good one! The soup is fantastic. The 1940s Citroen Van that sells it is very cool. But the philosophy behind it is kingdom class. Every soup bought buys a meal for a child in Kenya through Mary's Meals. J P is the founder. He is a member of our church family. He was a lawyer and he had a great future plotted out for him, but God got hold of his heart for this, for business and for justice. *Elephant Juice* was inspired by God, and at no stage did J P ask for permission. He just took a hill.

This is a call for you. If you lead in any facet of life, it is a call to a new quality and style of leadership. It's leadership of a different kind – kingdom leadership. Above all – it's a call to stand out boldness. It's a call to – take a step, stick out your neck and take to a hill – after all we are the sons of the Hill Maker. It's a challenge for your dream to become a scream!

We stand in a long line of bold sons and daughters. Luther's hill was the church and his stand was at a door. Martin Luther realised the church had become deeply corrupt and he nailed his 95 points of protest on the door of the church in Wittenberg. Savanarolla's hill was an abusive government and a stake. Savanarolla in pre-reformation Florence stood against the evil of the Medici family and the corruption of Rome. Martin Luther King's hill was Washington DC, a dream and an assassin's bullet.

My question is who in our generation will be written about in 200 years? If anyone is still here to write about us, that is, the Lord willing. Will it be anything like: 'The world is not worthy of you! God is not ashamed to be your God'?

A TIME TO SOW

We need churches planted of every shape and shade and style. We need to have lots of them – we need churches that will inspire in every aspect of culture to redeem and restore everything.

This world needs kingdom entrepreneurs who will speculate on what is given to them and they will make a difference. Our world needs the creativity and integrity that *Abba's* children bring to the table.

Ultimately, you and I have a choice: To hunker down – to escape the world – or else: to break out and love it!

Are we going to sit and spit out the pips of our pomegranate fruit? Will we satisfy ourselves with talk of victories of old and singing of assurance. Will we wait till he calls, or comes?

DOING IT IS DOING IT

Niki and I and a couple of friends spent some time recently, teaching and ministering to pastors and church planters in India. It was just such an eye-opening time. We were ministering and teaching and undoubtedly doing the majority of the learning.

The ministry of the Gospel amongst the Dalit people in India (250 million 'untouchables') is growing at an incredible rate. And it is this bold, faith-filled trust in the power of the Holy Spirit that is changing this nation. It's a very simple formula:

- You love people – practically.
- You free people – physically.
- You teach the Bible – simply.
- You tell people about Jesus liberally – and you pray for everything that moves!

It works. How do you plant a church in India? You just plant a church! How do you train someone to plant a church? You release them go plant a church! Doing it is doing it. Talking about it is talking about it. It requires boldness, faith and courage – it's hill-taking stuff!!

But in the Spirit, we can stand out!

TRIANGULATION

How do you find your hill? It's not rocket science. There's no looking for a needle in a haystack. God's will for your life is surprisingly broad, fully empowering, and highly dynamic. If you look to him, the Holy Spirit has a surprising way of making it clear. You have to find the triangulation point.

COMPLAINT

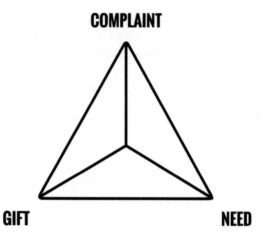

GIFT   NEED

A. **Your greatest complaint**. Vision flows out of complaint, more often than not. God will show you something. He will break your heart and you will believe that something is wrong.

B. **The world's greatest need?** You work it out.

C. **Your greatest gift.** If you don't know what this is, ask!

You can set in motion a series of necessary divine events.

- He gives you a *complaint*. Something you oppose. Something that needs to be better. Something that needs more.
- Then, if you ask him, he will give you a picture of what could be, *a vision*.
- If you press into this, he wants to give you a plan of how it could be, *a strategy*.
- At some stage, the vision will appear to die. This process is absolutely essential for reminding you of whose vision it is and for whose glory.
- And if you ask and work and cast this vision, He will surround you with a *team* who can make it be – we call that *missional church*.

This is the pattern and rhythm. It needs repeating and disturbing and responding. As you and I push deeper into attempting to embrace the kingdom in this world, we are constantly going to be disturbed by the Spirit in us. We'll jar and grate and grind up against value systems and practices and deeply held beliefs that grieve the heart of God.

This process is so important. Because bold men and women cast such a compelling vision that it eclipses the fear that followers may have. And releases the dreams that God has placed in hearts.. It acts, rather than just talks.

This process will ruin you for the ordinary, because it will propel us into living extraordinary kingdom lives. When you've tasted that, you will never want to go back. And in turn, you will inspire this process in others.

This is a time for armour bearers. This is a time to be bold. It's Jonathan's time, not Saul's! And our God is drawn to courage.

——————————————— SO: ———————————————

- Take an hour or so aside. What is your greatest complaint? What gets you upset, riles you?
- What is your gift? What do you dream of?
- Ask the Lord for vision. Share your dream with others, as many as you want. Invite one person to join your adventure, ask them to take the hill with you.

14.

KEEP LOW

Pride must die in you, or nothing of heaven can live in you.
Humility, Andrew Murray (1895)

•

As long as you are proud you cannot know God. A proud man is always looking down on things and people: and, of course, as long as you are looking down you cannot see something that is above you.
Mere Christianity, C S Lewis (1952)

•

And what does the LORD *require of you? To act justly and to love mercy and to walk humbly with your God.*
Micah 6:8

I want to tell you about a gift of immense value. It's a gift we can embrace and use. It's a gift which helps those who see it in us to see God himself. It is something that's chosen for us, instilled in us and valued deeply by Father God. Without it, you cannot stand. It's incredibly precious, even though it's rarely prized in Western culture, and the world doesn't have much time for it.

Humility is a standout quality. It's the secret to joy in life. It's the secret to harmony in relationships. It's the secret to deep peace with God. Humility is the heart and start of what it really means to build community. It's the driving force of what it takes to love people and reach people. You might think this is a huge statement to make. But stay with me.

We need to be bold. We need to be people of courage. We can believe all the right things and be really sound in our thinking and faith. We can have all the right goals and the finest of objectives. But if our methods and tactics, if our style and tone and volume are wrong – if we don't have humility – then boldness and courage will inevitably become destructive.

The result of courageous kingdom living is often great kingdom success. You'll see powerful breakthrough and supernatural signs and wonders. But without humility, great success brings real danger of damaging pride. And pride will destroy the kingdom in you – and in each and every one of us.

God encourages humility for good reason. It protects us, and it exalts him. It is the antidote to pride.

Pride is a great enemy. Pride was the diseased root of Satan's downfall – he wanted glory and power. Pride was clear in the hearts of the Pharisees. Humility is a great ally. Pride is about *my* glory. Humility is about the glory of Jesus. Pride is the compulsion to compare ourselves with others. Humility is comparing ourselves to Jesus. Pride is about independence. Humility is about dependence. Pride is the mother of all sin. Humility is the mother of all joy.

We live in a world that knows and exploits our pride – it anticipates, expects and even manipulates us through pride. The world – with all its advertising and promotion – knows we feel good when we look good. Pride doesn't have to try too hard to infect us – it has many subtle forms and we naturally give in to it. We have even brought it into the church. It's everywhere. We must stand against pride. We need, by the power of the Spirit, to tear it out of our lives, to crush it. And how do we crush it? We crush pride with humility. When we do this – when we fight pride with humility – transformation takes place.

Indeed it is this welding together of boldness and humility that is going to be transformational – for our churches and for our world.

We need to be bold. We are called to courage. We are equipped and encouraged to do incredible things, but we can't pursue a good thing in a bad way, then expect God to be pleased. We need to get some attitude. We need to practice the art of standing humbly-bold! That's what the Apostle Paul suggests in his letter to the Philippians. He encourages us to a tight alignment with Jesus' life; to imitate his attitude, and it is humility that he highlights.

> *Do nothing out of selfish ambition or vain conceit, but in humility consider others better than yourselves. Each of you should look not only to your own interests but also to the interests of others. Your attitude should be the same as that of Christ Jesus:*
> > *Who, being in very nature God,*
> > *did not consider equality with God something to be grasped, but rather made himself nothing, taking the very nature of a servant, being made in human likeness.*
> > *And being found in appearance as a man,*
> > *he humbled himself*
> > *and became obedient to death – even death on a cross!*
> > Philippians 2:3–8 (NIV 1984)

KEEP LOW

Jesus humbled himself. Get that. The word that is used here in the original is *tapeinoo*. It has the feel of voluntary humiliation and means 'not rising far from the ground'. Jesus kept low. He humbled himself. Let that sink in. The Author of Creation. There in the beginning. Lord of the Universe, enthroned, in heaven, God humbled himself. Being in very nature God, he humbled himself. God made himself nothing.

No-one shows more humility than Jesus. The Creator became creation. Omnipresent, he came to one place. He made himself nothing.

He wasn't born a king, though he could have been. He wasn't rich. He had no earthly status – he had nothing. He was the stable-born offspring of a teenage, unmarried mother. He grew up in a dodgy neighbourhood, of questionable heritage. It doesn't even appear that he had looks on his side. He had nowhere that he could call home. He faced rejection after rejection – even from those who truly loved him. He was crucified by those he came to serve. He experienced the most dreadful death, at the age of around thirty-three – in an insignificant corner of the Roman Empire.

And in doing this, he changed history.

If we want to participate with Jesus in his life and have the same results as Jesus then this is the way we must stand. And it will stand out magnificently.

Jesus never used his position as a power thing. His ability, his background, his potential, his talent. These were never used for status. He never once mentioned what he had given up. Jesus did not consider equality with God something to be grasped – even though he was God. He wasn't interested in status. Position didn't matter. Great earthly glory was not on his radar. It won't be for us either if we imitate Jesus' humility. Which is incredibly powerful. It's also incredibly liberating. It helps you be you.

Jesus made himself nothing. No reputation. No image. He wasn't concerned about being seen with the right people. In fact, he made a point of being seen with the wrong people. He accompanied tax collectors and prostitutes. He accompanies me. His image and what other people truly thought of him, really was of no importance to Jesus. It doesn't need to be for us.

Jesus said, 'Whoever wants to be first must take last place ...' Then he said, 'The kingdom of God belongs to those who are like children.' Also, he told us, 'The rulers of the Gentiles lord it over them. Not so with you.' There is no room in the Jesus life for standing on rights.

Ironically it is often in the life of the church itself where we see the danger of pride. I have seen obsession about position and title. Jealousy about others' gifts and service and success. I have known a desire to be with the right people, to be seen with the right people and to be on the right ministry row. I observe a growing culture of celebrity in the church at large.

Guys, let's *never* do it.

Let's not elevate people, let's not worship people. It dishonours God and endangers the hearts of his servants. The moment we begin to believe our own hype and our own power, we lose the heart of our anointing to be Jesus to this world.

There is no room in Jesus for superiority. If anyone had the right to display some superiority, it was Jesus, yet he didn't. There is only room for humility. It's nurtured by understanding who you really are and who Jesus is and then responding to that by imitating him.

If our attitude, our stand, is one of humility, then the way to achieve it is with intention. Intentionally.

SERVANTHOOD

Jesus took the very nature of a servant. Humility evidenced itself in servanthood. He made himself someone who always had time for people. Jesus' servanthood was about loving people – even when they let him down repeatedly. Loving Peter who would deny him. Loving James and John who wanted him to exalt them above others. Loving Judas, who he knew would betray him. Loving Thomas who would doubt him. Loving them, serving them and now doing the same for us.

Humility. Servanthood. Taking the lowest place.

Wanting the best for others. Preferring them. Putting ourselves out for those who might hardly notice us in return. Loving the unlovely. Doing the task that no-one else wants to do. That's our calling.

If the attitude is humility, it begins with obedience.

OBEDIENCE

The Jesus way was obedient to the Father. If you want to grow in your relationship with God, if you want to show the Lord you love him, if you want to be right in your relationship with others, here's how: obedience to the Father. The original meaning is to give ear to, to listen and obey. Obedience like Jesus showed. Simple, really. If you want bold humility, you'll find it through obedience.

You might be with me on this. But something may be troubling you. 'Obedient I get – but obedient to what? What is the Father calling me to do? I haven't heard his clear, un-ambiguous voice.'

I think you have. You start with obedience to things that are clear. No-brainer obedience!

As you practice this, things that are not so clear will become more obvious. You'll know when you're being prompted to obey. Get a grasp of the small stuff, and you'll soon be tackling the big stuff!

- When Jesus tells us that if we are out of relationship with our brother or sister, we need to go and sort it out – what part of that do we fail to understand?
- When God talks about what we are to do with our money and how we are to honour God with it – then we must do it.

- When the Bible makes clear that we are to love God and love people, we obey by working really hard at both.

These are just examples. You fill in others. Jesus was obedient to the Father. And those who would live the Jesus way will be as well.

Obedience doesn't always mean blessing for ourselves. Jesus was obedient to death – death on a cross. It was ghastly. But it was right and we've been immeasurably blessed because of it.

How can we clothe ourselves with humility, serve others and obey the Father? I think it's about seeing everything and every situation, and particularly our own lives, in the light of the person of Jesus. It's about putting every decision through the filter of the person of Jesus.

SACRIFICE

Crucifixion. The most brutal form of execution that this world has ever known. It's absolutely agonising. Inhumanely slow. It's completely humiliating.

The Son of God suffered this for us. He set his face, the Bible tells us, towards Jerusalem, towards the cross. He tackled it head on. He knew what this entailed – he sweated drops of blood over the stress of it. But he tackled it head on. He knew that this was the plan in the heart of the Father. And so he responded accordingly, and he went.

'Even death on a cross.'

So. Live every day in the light of the fact that we are sinners in need of the forgiveness of God. Know that forgiveness has been poured out on us. Constantly remind yourself that God loves you and your brothers and your sisters. Celebrate that his sacrifice is for you, and for me and for them. This truth is foundational for living in bold humility. Live for the applause of nail-scarred hands.

Look at Jesus and his majesty and come and worship. Bold humility flows from knowing you are on the winning team – you have nothing to prove and nothing to be afraid of. Live for his approval.

The graphic depiction of Christ's suffering and death, Mel Gibson's film *'The Passion of the Christ'* is brutal, at times gratuitous, and often stretches the narrative. Even so I encourage our leadership team to watch it – even annually. It may seem a little weird watching a film when you know the denouement. Like watching a re-run of a football match when someone has unhelpfully told you the score.

Watch *'The Passion'*, even though you know the ending. Actually, watch it BECAUSE you know the ending. Know that Jesus died on the cross for us and that he rose out of the tomb three days later. Know that he met with the disciples and that he then ascended into heaven. Know that God exalted him to the highest place. The one who died for me, the one who set me free, the one who forgave me and brought me into relationship with God, reigns. He reigns right now in the heavens. He mediates for me. He intercedes. He does it for me, and he does it for you. Know that.

Know that he who has the name Jesus, because he saves people, has also been given the name LORD, because he's in control. He's the Boss. What he says goes. Knowing this is crucial.

It means that however difficult it is in this life, we understand that there is coming a day, when he who is my Jesus, my lord, will be worshipped and honoured and glorified by all. Every knee shall bow and every tongue will confess that Jesus is Lord. All of heaven and all of earth will worship the one in whom I am putting my trust.

Understand that he, who is in me, demands more of me than selfish ambition. Understand that he, who is in me, is Lord. He is Lord and he calls us to humility and service and obedience. Knowing this changes everything. Suddenly, I want to lay down my life. I want to lay down my life because ... I get it.

LIVING WITH THE FOCUS ON JESUS

If he is Lord, you can't be. There's no room for two. This is so important because God hates pride and humiliates proud people. Read Proverbs 6:16–17 and Proverbs 16:5.

Even more than that, God *opposes* the proud. He opposes the proud, but he gives grace to the humble. He won't, he really won't bless the proud. But he gives grace to the humble. God loves bold humility.

So be humble, be really humble. Don't sell yourself, don't defend yourself, don't try and prove yourself, laugh at yourself. Celebrate other people's achievements. Obey God, serve people, follow Jesus.

Bold, humility.

Don't stand proud, don't stand tall – keep low. Stand bold, stand strong, but stand humble. Stand with humility of heart and life.

———————————— SO: ————————————

- Read Philippians 2. Slowly. Read Proverbs 6:5 and 16–17. Reflect on what they mean for your life.
- Take time to serve someone in a way that blesses them. Do something for someone that is a sacrifice for you. A radical one. Try to make it more than simply washing up the mugs in the office. Do a piece of great work and let a colleague take the credit for it. Or give up your Saturday morning to

look after someone's kids. And if you possibly can, do it on the quiet, don't let them know it was you.

- Then do it again.

You might also like to read:

The Power of Humility, R T Kendall (Muddy Pearl 2013)

STAND BACK

•

'Now then stand still and see this great thing the Lord is about to do before your eyes.'

Samuel 12:16

STAND. STAND UP AND STAND FIRM AND STAND OUT. AND THEN STAND BACK? NOT PRIMARILY BECAUSE YOUR JOB IS DONE. BUT BECAUSE THIS IS THE ESSENCE OF YOUR JOB, OUR TASK. TO MODEL A STAND, TO INSPIRE A STAND AND TO MAKE A WAY AND SPACE FOR MANY STAND TO HAPPEN. YOU SEE IF WE STAND IN WELL, STAND UP WELL, STAND FIRM WELL AND STAND OUT AS WE ARE SUPPOSED TO. AND THEN STAND BACK WE HAVE THE POTENTIAL OF CAUSING A STANDING EPIDEMIC THAT WILL CHANGE THE WORLD.

15.

YOLO?

Aye, fight and you may die. Run, and you'll live... at least a while. And dying in your beds, many years from now, would you be willin' to trade ALL the days, from this day to that, for one chance, just one chance, to come back here and tell our enemies that they may take our lives, but they'll never take ... OUR FREEDOM!

Braveheart, Mel Gibson (1995)

•

The fear of death follows from the fear of life. A man who lives fully is prepared to die at any time.

Mark Twain (1835–1910)

•

What good is it for someone to gain the whole world, yet forfeit their soul?

Mark 8:36

•

A good person leaves an inheritance for their children's children, but a sinner's wealth is stored up for the righteous.

Proverbs 13:22

Maybe I'm past it? A dinosaur who loves macs just because they are pretty but would prefer a decent pen and a quality journal. But I just can't get used to text language. I am not your M8. In fact I'm not speaking to you if you insist on using numbers where letters should be. I think LOL means 'lots of love' and I don't want to meet you L8TR. The phrase that gets me most, however, is YOLO. Not because I don't understand it, ('you only live once') or because I don't get it ('grab at life'; 'go for it') but because it sums up and epitomises the tendency in the rising generation to immediacy, entitlement and superficiality. Don't hear me wrong – this is not the rantings of a grumpy old man. It's just that there is so much more. And we are part of a far, staggeringly far, bigger story. It started before us and it will probably go on way beyond us.

We all carry a legacy.

In more ways than you might imagine. What you bequeath to the next generation is being worked out right now. It works out for good, or ill, for ordinary, or extra-ordinary. We all carry legacies.

If you live from your God-given identity, then you carry that. And if you carry a God-given identity, you have the incredible capacity to pass that on.

If you deal with your stuff – your issues, your challenges, your brokenness – if you deal with these, and you stop living out of your broken identity, then you have the wonderful freedom of knowledge that you won't pass those issues on to those who follow.

If you carry boldness and humility; if you carry forgiveness and community and really live it; if you carry intimacy and everyone knows it; if you carry these things, it is very likely that you will pass these on.

Now that would be quite a legacy.

WAYS AND INTENTIONS

The only way to leave this grace legacy is intentionally. Read Luke 5:27 and Luke 6:12–13. Jesus calls his disciples to him. They are not yet a small group, but faces in a large crowd. He chooses twelve. Why did Matthew follow? Matthew followed because Jesus asked him. How did the twelve become the twelve? Because Jesus picked them.

There is a huge principle illustrated here. The secret to strong, God-honouring, generational leadership is intentional apprenticeship. Intentional succession. At the very outset of Jesus' ministry, before he had launched, if you like, he chose the very people he would hand the whole thing on to. Not in Gethsemane, not on the Cross, but the first thing he did. His first priority.

Success depends upon succession.

It is fascinating in the life of Jesus, that choosing and training his successors was almost the first thing on his agenda. It is also fascinating that Jesus banked on raw potential rather than waiting for the finished article. He saw beyond the person's current state into who they truly were and who they were becoming.

Let's face it, none were anywhere close to being up to the task.

Peter was frequently wrong, but never in doubt. He had persistent foot-in-mouth disease. He was impulsive, reactionary and had a temper he could barely control. Let's not even mention the denial thing! Yet he is called to lead the church. James and John had superiority issues. They had mother issues and were not called the 'sons of thunder' because they were good at weather forecasting. Simon was a terrorist. Nathaniel barely features at all – he gets so little mention that you probably aren't even sure he was one of the twelve. And Judas? He was trusted to look after the money.

They weren't the pick of the bunch.

But Jesus poured himself into all twelve, and in particular three, and they were all so different.

Peter. He was a northern fisherman, not short of an opinion. In fact Peter was blunt to the point of offence at times. He was physical. He lopped off a Roman soldier's ear in such a way to suggest that it wasn't the first time he'd taken a weapon to someone. The Gospel he inspires (Mark) begins – and hear this in a Northern English accent – 'The beginning of the Gospel about Jesus Christ, the Son of God.' Peter called a spade a spade! If he had played rugby, Peter would have been a cauliflower-eared forward!

John. Very different from Peter. Enigmatic. Poetic. Mystic. Philosophical. You need to hear John's Gospel read in an eccentric, distracted Oxbridge accent. Think tousled hair, tweed jacket with leather patches. 'In the beginning was the Word and the Word was with God and the Word was God. He was with God in the beginning.'

James. I would love to tell you about James but I can't, because we just don't know much about him.

Jesus picked this band of misfits and ragamuffins to live out his legacy. And in doing so, he modelled what we must do.

If we are to leave a God-honouring legacy we must give ourselves to nurturing, mentoring and doing our bit to release the huge variety of gifts and callings of the rising generation. We need to apprentice others intentionally. We need to enable people to learn what we have learnt. We need to share what we are still learning. We need to do this so that they can do what we have done and will do – only better!

Jesus was not a one-man band. He never considered doing ministry alone. So, we need to spend ourselves in discipling and coaching, resourcing and releasing. This must become a natural part of life's rhythm. We need to pass on what we have, to give it away.

I am so grateful to those who took risks with me. I had a father who always encouraged the God-given gifts in me. He taught me to preach and let me have his pulpit. With grace, and patience, he sat through the youthful, passionate rants of a young man who thought he knew so much! I am so thankful for my first boss, David – a senior pastor, who, if he had issues of insecurity, hid them brilliantly. He let me preach more than he should have done. He let me lead more than I was ready to. He continually encouraged and nurtured the vision that God had placed inside me. He never attempted to stub it out – even though I would get him into hot water every now and then.

I love excellence. I think that in everything that we attempt in church, we should go for kingdom class – that's way beyond world class, let alone first class – but there is something more important than getting things right. Most important is enabling kingdom in the long term. We can do this intentionally, apprenticing people so that they in turn, will apprentice others.

Identify and invest.

Invest in those who are following your lead. Be practical about that. Breakfast and lunch with those who you are attempting to pour yourself into. Whenever you are doing what you do really well, do it in front of those who are learning to do what you do well.

HONING IN THE WHITE HEAT

Having identified the guys that he would pass the whole thing on to, Jesus then began to invest in their lives. In fact, a significant proportion of Jesus' teaching and miracles were as much about teaching them his ministry as anything else. Jesus was practically and effectively demonstrating what it means to minister this kingdom. He took them immediately on a mission trip, knowing this is how they would grow best. Interestingly, he did not send them to a scholar to work for a three-year qualification. Nor did he send them into the desert for solitude. Jesus knew that their discipleship, calling and anointing would be honed best in the white heat of missional ministry.

Jesus apprentices them. He pours into them. Then, he unequivocally passes the whole thing on to them.

John 20. Jesus makes it clear. The Father has sent me, and is in all that you saw in me and from me. What you've seen of my anointing and of my commission – was only doing what the Father has said. I operated in the power of the Holy Spirit. Now – you go and do likewise. Here's the power. Here comes the authority. Go and do likewise!

There is nothing new for us here, and yet that's not the way we tend to do it. Strong leaders tend to hang onto leadership. Many Christian organisations, conferences and movements tend to have the same leadership for generations. The result of this is that vision stagnates.

Churches don't naturally buy into succession policy. A pastor with a seemingly successful ministry might lead a church for thirty years, but have no succession plan. When he leaves, the church then wallows for three years, during which the search committee work out that the Archangel Gabriel is not available, (apparently he already has a job). They then appoint the best person they can find, who subsequently changes everything. During this time, momentum is lost and one quarter of the devoted membership leaves. If not physically, they leave in their hearts.

We need to leave a legacy. And one that has been intentionally crafted.

The evidence of a failure to do this is all around. We've seen it in the demise of the church in our nation. We've seen whole generations of our young people go elsewhere. They've played football and gone shopping on their Sundays because it was more fun. Because it meant more to them. There, they could really participate. There, they could really belong. At football they felt needed. They were part of team. When shopping they felt valued and wanted.

Young men and women found other arenas to throw themselves, their gifts and their creativity into. This can sometimes bring good – lots of good. God-pleasing things got started. But the Church of Jesus Christ, his beloved bridegroom, increasingly looked obsolete and was starved of this creative passion.

Some young people planted and led their own expressions of church. Often this was out of hurt and pain and even rebellion. Sometimes that worked. It worked because Father God can redeem all things.

Indeed many have been wonderful examples of the power of God at work. But so often things birthed in the wrong way have a habit of facing significant challenges later in development.

STEWARDSHIP, OR OWNERSHIP?

This ministry, this gift, this calling: it's not ours. We have it on trust. Quite simply, it belongs to God. It is to be used for his glory and is to be passed on with generosity and ease to the next generation. It is his church, not mine. His gift, not mine. His calling, not mine. I hold it lightly and I pass it on gladly. It's not about protection – it's about permission.

So, our story at Central is that we are committed, as a core value, to the practice of discipleship, of missional apprenticeship. It is an amazing privilege to be able to apprentice people. It is necessary.

As we intentionally practice legacy leaving, we have two principles and two programmes.

PRINCIPLES : THE CULTURE OF APPRENTICESHIP

This needs to be holistic. It's not that we are just running a discipleship programme for the spiritually elite. This culture needs to permiate every area of church life and for us it means specific things:

- *All in.* Firstly, our ambition is that every member of staff, every elder, every senior leader, is apprenticing someone else – you apprentice what you do well. So, I apprentice those whom I suspect to have gifts of teaching and of visionary leadership. I apprentice those with an apostolic gift. I share with them who I am and what I do. Our Discipleship Pastor apprentices those who have gifts of training others, those whose calling is to encourage and enable body ministry.

- *All age.* Secondly, we integrate generations. We expect that if we are to exist in a culture of apprenticeship then whatever way you cut the church, it should bleed apprenticeship. We start young, with the desire that our children, our young people, are being released into their giftings and encouraged to minister now. We watch them learning and growing in their ability to hear from God, and their abilities to minister to others and to lead from where they are. Whatever age, or stage. We refuse to completely divide our children's ministry off from the rest of the church programme. However large we grow, we will not countenance this. We need our children to be exposed to what God is doing with the rest of us and more than that we need to be exposed to what our children bring to our community. In truth, the most powerful times of healing ministry in our gatherings have been when the children have been the prayer team.

- *Prejudice towards the young.* We intentionally start young and disproportionally invest in youth. This is not always warmly appreciated but it is for good reason. When you work with young people you get to be a potter. You work with clay. If it goes wrong you pick up the clay and start again. The material is malleable and forgiving, eventually something beautiful can be formed. As people get older working with them is still important but it is more the domain of the sculptor. Something beautiful can still be formed. But rather than working with hands alone, a hammer and chisel are needed. That which is chipped off is lost in the often painful process of remodelling. Start forming legacy young.

PROGRAMMES

Leadership/Discipleship

As I have mentioned, every year, Niki and I identify twelve emerging leaders, who we would love to pour ourselves into. We attempt to invest in, release, and equip a fresh generation of leaders. If twelve was good enough for Jesus, it seems good enough for us.

This group meets at our house once a week. They are welcomed into the family. We study leadership principles and spiritual disciplines. Disciples are encouraged to use journals. To memorise Scripture and minister to one another. We fast every week and break that fast together. The aim is that this pattern of living will become habit forming. This group becomes a safe place to take risks and to grow in faith. These groups become family for us.

Apprentice Pastors

We offer a year programme for those who feel called to be missional leaders of this thing we call church. We invite those that we hand pick and have already invested in, to come and serve and shadow and run with the dreams God has placed in their hearts. We do this on the basis that we are called to replicate ourselves as individuals and as church. Indeed we are just not convinced that we can go to many of the training institutes in our nation and pick someone off the shelf, who comes with the right DNA. We need to be equipping leaders. We need men and women of Issachar and men and women of Zebulun.

'men of Issachar, who understood the times and knew what Israel should do ... Men of Zebulun, experienced soldiers prepared for battle with every type of weapon, to help David with undivided loyalty'

1 Chronicles 12:32–33

- We want to train our apprentices in leadership and discernment.
- We want to train our apprentices in cultural awareness and to live counter-cultural lifestyles.
- We want to train our apprentices in visionary leadership.
- We want to train our apprentices in sane spiritual warfare.
- We want to encourage our apprentices in loyalty.

Our desire is to train apprentices who will plant and pastor churches. Apprentices who will pioneer kingdom ministries. Apprentices who will start and lead businesses. Apprentices who will transform every aspect of culture and bring restoration to all things. Men and women immersed in the Word. Equipped by the Spirit – kingdom leaders.

One day I will have had my earth time. There will be a coffin in a church and in it will be my shell, not me. Personally I hope that thousands turn up to my funeral. (If you don't show, I will know!) There will be a service and then food, maybe even Scottish dancing. I want it recorded now: there won't be any quiche, but there'll definitely be those small sausages on sticks. Materially, I will leave ... not a lot. A really nice set of TaylorMade golf clubs. There'll be thousands of sermons. I probably will never have owned my vintage VW beetle. Or a city centre loft apartment with stripped wood floors. Materially, I won't leave much. My hope, my prayer, is that I will leave thousands of sons and daughters in the faith. Men and women who really lived. People whose transformation changed the world. Stand out people.

That's the true meaning of legacy. We all leave one, and how that's shaped depends on how we live. We have the potential, through

Father God, to leave an awesome legacy. To do so you've got to stand back.

―――――――――――――――― SO: ――――――――――――――――

- Fifty years from now – you are gone, well gone, with Jesus gone. Sitting on the sofa are your grandkids, discussing you. What do you want them to say, what did you live for, what would you like to see in them that you passed on?

- Who are your spiritual children? How are you investing in them? What do you hope they will accomplish? What is the vision you have for life? Write it out. Dare to share it with someone else.

- And what if that coffin time was relatively soon? What if you knew you had three years left? What do you stop doing? What do you start doing? How do you take your stand?